# A GLOSSARY OF
# ENGLISH GRAMMAR

# A Glossary of
# English Grammar

*Geoffrey Leech*

Edinburgh University Press

© Geoffrey Leech, 2006

Edinburgh University Press Ltd
22 George Square, Edinburgh

Typeset in Sabon
by Norman Tilley Graphics, Northampton,
and printed and bound in Finland
by WS Bookwell

A CIP record for this book is
available from the British Library

ISBN-10 0 7486 2406 6 (hardback)
ISBN-13 978 0 7486 2406 5
ISBN-10 0 7486 1729 9 (paperback)
ISBN-13 978 0 7486 1729 6

The right of Geoffrey Leech
to be identified as author of this work
has been asserted in accordance with the
Copyright, Designs and Patents Act 1988.

Published with the support of the Edinburgh
University Publishing Initiatives Fund.

A70145

# Contents

# Use of special symbols

A **bold** typeface within an entry shows a cross-reference to another entry. Major cross-references are often at the end of an entry.

*Italics* are used to represent an English example or word used for illustration.

***Bold italics***, when they occur as part of an example, are meant to highlight or emphasize that part of the example.

***Bold italics*** also refer to a verb as if in a dictionary, where the different verb forms are irrelevant. (For example, ***look*** means *look/looks/looked/looking*.)

~    A swung dash indicates a relation between alternative forms of the same basic word or pattern, for example: *boy ~ boys*.

( )    Round brackets in examples indicate something which is optional, that is, can be omitted or ignored.

[ ]    For clarity, square brackets are sometimes used in examples to signal the boundaries of a major constituent, usually a clause.

|    Vertical lines in examples are sometimes used to separate main elements of a clause, for example: subject, verb phrase and object.

\*    An asterisk before an example indicates that the example is unacceptable as a piece of English.

*Note*
The terminology in this book is mainly based on that of Randolph Quirk et al. (1985): *A Comprehensive Grammar of the English Language* – see the Introduction.

# Introduction

This book is a concise glossary of terms (words, expressions) used to describe English grammar. The book could have been much longer – and much more intimidating. This would have taken me into the territory of dictionary-making rather than glossary-making. To avoid this, I have had to choose rather carefully which are the more important words to include and which terms can be excluded.

Like other fields of knowledge, grammar suffers from overlapping and coinciding terminologies. For example, far too often different grammarians provide different terms for describing the same thing. In part this may be for a good reason: different grammarians use different terms because they are looking at the same thing from a different viewpoint – wearing different theoretical glasses, shall we say.

But there is an additional reason why terminology proliferates in the study of grammar. There is not one undivided 'community of English grammarians', who talk to one another and exchange ideas in a single forum. (If there were, we could hope that they would get together and try to standardize their terminology.) Rather, in broad terms, there are three communities. There is a community of *grammar teachers* – people who are interested in grammar from a pedagogical point of view. There is a community of *theoretical researchers*, who are primarily interested in English grammar as an exemplar of human language. And, between these two, there is a middle-of-the-road body of *descriptive grammarians*, people who are interested in giving an account of English grammar as a goal in itself.

It should not be supposed that these people always disagree. On the contrary, they do share a lot of terminology and use much of it in the same way or in similar ways. For example, a noun is a 'noun' and a clause is a 'clause' in virtually every grammatical account of English. But there are some areas where their terminology differs unnecessarily. Teachers of grammar generally use the term 'continuous' for the *be* + *ing*-form construction of the verb, as in *is reading, was telling*, whereas descriptive grammarians and theoretical researchers use the term 'progressive'. On the other hand, the term 'agreement' is more likely to be used in theoretical grammar, as compared with 'concord' which is found more in descriptive and teaching grammars. (This term is used for cases where grammar requires matching choices, like the choice of *eats* after *A rabbit* and *eat* after *Rabbits* in: *A rabbit eats grass* and *Rabbits eat grass*.)

Because of such differences, this glossary contains more than a few cross-reference entries of the following pattern: 'X: another term for Y'. The opposite case, where the same term is used by different specialists for different, incompatibly defined concepts, is another bugbear of grammar, and where necessary I have represented this by definitions with different index numbers, e.g. 'complement(1)' and 'complement(2)'.

Given such differences, it is reasonable for a glossary like this one to focus on a 'middle-of-the-road' descriptive approach, capitalizing on the theory-neutral common ground of grammatical terminology, while including additional terms and definitions where they are important. For this purpose, I have chosen as my default grammar framework the one to be found in the authoritative reference grammar R. Quirk et al., *A Comprehensive Grammar of the English Language* (Longman, 1985) and in other grammars from the same stable – e.g. Greenbaum and Quirk (1990) and Leech and Svartvik (2002).

My earlier characterization of grammar terminology as belonging to three different communities was an oversimplification. It is better, I suggest, to see the relation between the three communities as scalar, with the theoretical and pedagogical grammars at different ends of the spectrum and descriptive grammars somewhere in the middle. This is partly because descriptive grammars themselves differ in their positions on this scale. A recent self-proclaimed descriptive grammar, R. Huddleston and G. Pullum's admirably comprehensive *Cambridge Grammar of the English Language* (2002), has a stronger theoretical orientation than Quirk et al. (1985), and also sometimes labels grammatical concepts with new terms that are less widely accepted than the more traditional ones. I have not neglected this important grammar's terminology, but have not made it the main focus of the book.

At the more theoretical end of the scale, there are many competing theories of grammar which to a greater or lesser extent develop their own terminologies. These cannot be included in this book, but it is worth pointing out that even the some of the major grammatical categories which are the common ground of different theories have different labels attached to them in different frameworks. The systemic functional grammar framework of M. A. K. Halliday has a terminological tradition of its own, and adheres to terms like nominal group and verbal group instead of the more widely used noun phrase and verb phrase. I have included these two Hallidayan terms, but in general the terminology specific to that framework is not covered by this book. My aim has been to concentrate on widely used theory-neutral terms, where these exist.

Even more than is usual for glossaries, the present glossary relies on cross-references (in **bold** typeface) between one entry and another. Such cross-referencing is especially important for grammatical terms, because grammar forms a fairly tight system of mutually defining concepts. If we take a fairly basic grammatical term like 'clause', it is remarkable that (a) to describe a clause thoroughly we need to refer to many other grammatical terms; and (b) To define many other terms, we need to refer to clauses. Nevertheless, I have avoided using **bold** typeface on every occasion where a term defined elsewhere in the glossary occurs in some entry. In particular, basic and well-known terms such as 'verb', 'noun', 'clause', 'sentence' are often taken for granted and are not highlighted in bold whenever they occur in entries for other terms.

A glossary of English grammar depends heavily on illustrations. In practice, these can be short examples of no more than a few words each. However, it is important that such examples be convincing and natural, and for this purpose I have often extracted and adapted data from electronic corpora representative of real English speech and writing. These include the Brown Corpus and Freiburg-Brown Corpus of American English, the Lancaster-Oslo-Bergen (LOB) and Freiburg-Lancaster-Oslo-Bergen (FLOB) Corpora of British English and the British National Corpus. Details of these can be found at the following web addresses: http://khnt.hit.uib.no/icame/manuals/ and http://www.natcorp.ox.ac.uk. I have also taken a few examples from a grammar book particularly rich in authentic examples, D. Biber et al. (1999), *Longman Grammar of Spoken and Written English* (1999).

At the end of the glossary I have added a section on suggested reading, referring to a preceding list of useful books related to English grammar. In general, I have restricted this list to books which are not too difficult for the non-specialist. Many of them are books for students and teachers; a few are for the general public interested in matters of language. This book is a revised, updated and much expanded version of the author's *Introducing English Grammar* (Penguin, 1992).

Geoffrey Leech
Lancaster University
July 2005

**abstract noun**   A **noun** which refers to an abstraction, that is which does not refer to anything physical or concrete. Common types of abstract noun are (a) nouns referring to events, actions or states, such as *arrival, invitation, hope*; (b) nouns referring to qualities, such as *happiness, size, absurdity*; (c) nouns referring to mental or perceptual phenomena, such as *idea, music, vision*. Abstract nouns contrast with **concrete nouns**, such as *window, student* and *steam*, which refer to physically identifiable entities or substances. Like concrete nouns, abstract nouns can be **count, non-count** or both. For example, *arrival* is count (as the plural form *arrivals* shows), *happiness* is non-count (as the oddity of *\*happinesses* shows), and *vision* can be both: *We need vision* and *We need visions* are both possible, but with a difference of meaning.

Many abstract nouns are derived from **verbs** (for example, *arrive ~ arrival, invite ~ invitation*), or derived from **adjectives** (for example, *happy ~ happiness, wide ~ width*). Such derived nouns are typically recognizable by their suffixes (for example, *-ation, -ion, -ness, -ity, -ance, -ence, -hood, -ing, -al*). Some, however, have exactly the same form as a corresponding verb (for example, *hope, love, release, mention*).

**accusative case**   An alternative term for **objective case**.

**active, active voice**   The term applied to a verb phrase which is

not passive, or to a clause which contains such a verb phrase.
(See **passive; voice**.)

**actor**   see **agent**[2]

**adjectival clause**   A term sometimes used for a clause which, like
an **adjective**, modifies a **noun**, for example a **relative clause**.
Compare: *an expensive present* (where *expensive* is an adjective)
with *a present which cost a lot* (where *which cost a lot* is a relative clause).

**adjective**   Adjectives are a large class of words (for example,
*good, bad, new, accurate, careful*) which define more precisely
the reference of a **noun** or **pronoun**. A typical adjective can occur
before a noun, as in *a good plan, this bad weather, our new
manager, accurate predictions*. (In this position, the adjective is
said to premodify the head of a **noun phrase**.) A typical adjective
can also occur after the verb *be*, as in *The plan was risky;
The weather is bad; Your predictions were inaccurate*. (In this
position, the adjective is said to be the **complement**, or **subject
complement**.) Most common adjectives can follow degree
adverbs such as *very* (for example, *very good, very accurate*) and
can also be used in a **comparative** form such as *better, older,
more accurate*, or in a **superlative** from such as *best, oldest,
most accurate*. Many of these **gradable** adjectives form their
comparative and superlative forms with the *-er* and *-est* suffixes,
for example *cold ~ colder ~ coldest*. Whereas these statements
define 'typical' adjectives, many adjectives fail to match one or
more of these criteria: *asleep* cannot be used in front of a noun,
and *sole* (as in *the sole survivor*) cannot be used after the verb *be*.
Most common adjectives form pairs which contrast in terms of
meaning: *good ~ bad, wide ~ narrow, useful ~ useless*, and so
on. Many adjectives are derived from other words (especially
nouns), and are easy to recognize by their suffixes. Some of the
most common adjective suffixes are: *-al* (as in *equal*), *-ous* (as in
*famous*), *-ic* (as in *basic*), *-y* (as in *sleepy*), *-ful* (as in *beautiful*)
and *-less* (as in *hopeless*).

**adjective phrase**    An adjective phrase is a **phrase** in which an **adjective** is the head or main word. The simplest kind of adjective phrase is one which consists simply of an adjective, as in *The meeting was noisy*. An adjective phrase can be made more complex by adding modifiers (especially **degree adverbs**) before the adjective: *The meeting was very/too noisy*. Also, the adjective can be followed by other words which modify or complement the meaning of the adjective: *too poor to feed themselves*; *too early for breakfast*; *useful enough*; *funnier than the last show*; and so on. An adjective phrase can contain a **comparative clause**, as in *The weather this winter has been colder than I can remember*. In terms of their function, adjective phrases generally act as complements: either as **subject complement**[1], as in *The meeting was too long*, or as **object complement**[1], as in *I found the meeting too long*.

**adjunct**    An adjunct is an element which is part of a **clause** or sentence in which it modifies the verb (or the verb plus other elements). Adjunct is another term for **adverbial**, but its use is often limited to adverbials which are closely integrated with the rest of the clause, for example adverbials of time, of place, of manner, of instrument and so on, as in *They then attacked me*; *They attacked me in the street*; *They attacked me fiercely*; *They attacked me with knives*; and so on. Adjuncts are generally optional parts of the sentence, but in certain cases adjuncts cannot be omitted, for example the adjunct of place in *She put the book on the shelf*. Compare **linking adverbial**; **sentence adverbial**.

**adnominal**    A term sometimes used to describe elements of a **noun phrase** other than the **head**. Modifiers and determiners in a noun phrase are therefore adnominal.

**adverb**    Adverbs are a major class of words, mainly consisting of words which modify verbs, adjectives and other adverbs, for example adverbs of time (*now*, *then* and so on), of place (*there*, *somewhere* and so on), of manner (*well*, *carefully* and so on), of degree (*so*, *very* and so on), and a wide range of other words which do not fit into such easily defined categories: *just*, *either*, *however*, *actually* and so on. Adverbs form a disparate set of words; in fact, some grammarians have doubted the viability of the adverb class. There is a fairly major distinction, for example, between words capable of taking an adverbial function in the clause (for example, *then*, *there*, *quickly*, *much*) and degree words capable of premodifying other words such as adjectives, adverbs, and determiners (for example *very* in *very large*, *very quickly* and *very many*). However, these subclasses overlap considerably. Another way of dividing the class of adverbs into distinct categories is to separate a **closed class** of function words (*now*, *where*, *so*, *too*, *just* and so on) and an **open class** of derived words, chiefly adverbs in *-ly* (for example, *quickly*, *saliently*, *refreshingly*). Some adverbs (for example, *long*, *early*, *later*) are identical in form to adjectives to which they are also closely related in meaning. (See **adverbial; modifier.**)

**adverb phrase**    A phrase containing an **adverb** as the main word, or head. An adverb phrase may consist of one word (an adverb alone), as in *She hits the ball **hard***, or of two words, as in *She hits the ball **extremely hard*** (where *hard* is modified by another adverb, *extremely*), or of a longer sequence of words, as in *Success had not come **as easily as they had hoped***. (See **adverb.**)

**adverbial**    An element of a **clause** or sentence which adds extra meaning about the event or state of affairs described. Adverbials are the most peripheral of the clause elements **subject** (S), **verb phrase** (V), **object** (O), **complement** (C) and **adverbial** (A) which make up the structure of a clause. Adverbials are normally optional. That is, they can be omitted without changing the relations of meaning and structure in the rest of the clause. *Suddenly* is optional in *She left **suddenly*** (compare *She left*). Adverbials are also typically mobile – that is, they can occur in more than one position in the clause, as in *She left **suddenly** ~*

*She suddenly left ~ Suddenly she left.* A further point about adverbials is that more than one of them can occur in the same clause. This clause contains three: *At midnight, she secretly left to meet Heathcliff.* Adverbials belong to varied meaning categories, for example adverbials of time-when, of duration, of frequency, of place, of manner, of means, of instrument, of degree, of purpose. In many cases, these categories can be distinguished as answering different question words (*when, where, how, why*) or question phrases (*how long, how often, how much, how far*):

> When did she leave? *At midnight.*
> How did she leave? *Secretly.*
> Why did she leave? *To meet Heathcliff.*

Despite their name, adverbials do not necessarily contain adverbs: they may consist of an **adverb phrase**, as in *She left (very) suddenly,* but they may also take the form of a **prepositional phrase** (*at midnight, through the window*), or of a **noun phrase** (*last night, the week before last*), or of an **adverbial clause** (*as soon as she could*).

**adverbial clause**    A clause that acts as an **adverbial** in the main clause or sentence it belongs to. Adverbial clauses can be said to modify the rest of the main clause – that is, they add extra information in terms of time, condition, concession, cause or reason, result and so on. In *She suddenly left when the police entered the building,* the adverbial clause *when the police entered the building* tells us more about the circumstances in which she left: it is an adverbial of time, answering the question *When did she leave?* While acting as an adverbial in the main clause, the adverbial clause also contains its own clause elements: *the police* (**subject**), *entered* (**verb phrase**) and *the building* (**object**). In addition, most adverbial clauses begin with a **conjunction**, signalling their link with the main clause. Examples of such conjunctions are *when, since, before, after, until, as, while* (conjunctions of time); *if, unless* (conditional conjunctions); *although, though* (concessive conjunctions); *because, as, since* (conjunctions of cause or reason). Like other adverbials, adverbial clauses are typically mobile, and can occur either before or after the other elements of the main clause. Compare:

You should lie down [*if you feel ill*].
[*If you feel ill*], you should lie down.

Adverbial clauses are varied in structure as well as in meaning. For example, there are different kinds of **non-finite** adverbial clause:

I opened the window [*to let in some fresh air*].
[*Queuing up for lunch*], Ricky felt sick as a dog.
[*Flanked by four huge minions,*] he was making a lot of noise.

(See **adverbial; subordinate clause.**)

**affirmative**    Affirming the truth of some statement. An affirmative clause or sentence is one that is both declarative and positive, for example: *He ran up the stairs*, in contrast to *He didn't run up the stairs* or *Did he run up the stairs?*

**agent**    This term has two different, though related, meanings.
    (1) An agent is a noun phrase (or sometimes, a noun clause) following *by* in a passive construction, and corresponding to the subject of an active clause: in *Several children were rescued **by the police**, the police* is the agent. Compare *the police* as the subject of an active clause: *The police rescued several children.* An agent typically refers to the 'doer' of an action signalled by the verb (see (2) below). But in some passive constructions, the agent is not a 'doer', that is does not identify the performer of an action: in *The crime was seen on television **by millions of people***, the spectators the agent refers to are not doing anything, but simply keeping their eyes open. The agent of a passive verb is frequently omitted: *Several children were rescued. The mystery has been solved.* (See **passive voice.**)
    (2) The term agent is also used semantically to indicate the

'doer' of an action, as contrasted with the 'doee' – the person, thing and so on to which something happens. Thus nouns such as *employer*, *teacher* and *manager*, referring to the 'doer' of a certain task or role, are often called 'agent nouns'.

**agentless passive**    A **passive** construction that has no **agent**[1], also called a 'short passive'. For example: *Two suspects have been arrested*.

**agreement**    Another term for **concord**.

**alternative question**    A question where the speaker offers the hearer a closed choice between two or more alternative possibilities: *Is the kitten male or female? Would you like orange juice, grapefruit juice or tomato juice?* The word *or* signals the relation between the alternatives. Unlike *yes-no* **questions**, alternative questions normally end with a falling intonation contour. There are also reported alternative questions: these are subordinate **nominal clauses** (or **complement clauses**) where the alternatives are expressed by *whether . . . or . . .* (*If* can replace *whether* here.) *They asked her whether/if the kitten was male or female. Maria wondered whether/if he was waving or drowning.* (See **question**; **reported speech**.)

**anacoluthon** (plural: **anacolutha**)    A sudden change from one grammatical construction to another in the middle of a sentence. For example: *Why don't you – okay, just do what you like.*

**antecedent**    An expression to which a pronoun refers (or – more properly – makes **coreference**) and which normally precedes the pronoun in the text. The term antecedent is used primarily for the noun or nominal expression which precedes a relative pronoun such as *who* or *which*. For example, in *the girl who had a heart transplant*, *(the) girl* is the antecedent of *who*. Sometimes the antecedent is a whole clause or sentence: *Then Pip dropped the ball in the soup bowl, which made me laugh*. (Here the antecedent of *which* is *(Then) Pip dropped the ball in the soup bowl*.) The term antecedent also applies to an expression to which a personal pronoun such as *he*, *she*, *it* or *they* cross-refers: *Sinbad told the queen he had lost all his possessions*. (Here *he* and *his* refer to Sinbad, so *Sinbad* is their antecedent.) Yet another extended use of the term is to apply it to an expression which follows the pronoun rather than precedes it. For example, *Marie* is the antecedent of *her* in *To her own family, Marie was just an ordinary girl*. (See **corefer, coreference, coreferential**; **personal pronouns; relative clause; sentence relative clause**.)

*any*-words     see **non-assertive**

**apposition** (adjective: **appositive**)     A relation between two constituents such that the following statements normally apply: (a) apposition exists between two **noun phrases**; (b) the two constituents in apposition are in a relationship which could be expressed by the verb *be*; (c) the two constituents are juxtaposed and combined in a single noun phrase, which can act, for example, as **subject** or **object** of a sentence. Examples of apposition are: *George Washington, first President of the USA*; *My neighbour Mrs Randall*; *tequila, a powerful Mexican drink*. By extension, the term apposition can apply to a noun phrase next to a coreferential **nominal clause** (for example, *the idea/hope that the White House would change its policy* can become a sentence with *be*: *The idea/hope was that the White House would change its policy*). An *of*-phrase in which *of* links **coreferential** expressions may also be termed appositive: *the city of Beirut*; *the disgrace of losing the contest*.

**appositive**     see **apposition**

**articles**     The two words *the* and *a* (*an* before vowels), known respectively as the definite article and the indefinite article. They are the most common English **determiners**, beginning a **noun phrase** and typically followed by a **noun**, with or without **modi-**

fiers: *the picture, a picture, the actor, an actor, a brilliant actor.* Normally, **proper nouns** (names) do not have a preceding article (*Paris, John, Congress*). Moreover, **plural** and **non-count** nouns do not have an indefinite article: *the pictures* contrasts with *pictures* in *I like the pictures ~ I like pictures.* Similarly, *I like the music* contrasts with *I like music.* In the case of **common nouns**, absence of *the*, as in *I like music*, is frequently regarded as an instance of the **zero article**. This is because it is useful, from some points of view, to regard the initial determiner as obligatory for English noun phrases, so that the absence of *the* is itself a mark of indefiniteness. (See also **definite article; indefinite article; zero article.**)

aspect  A grammatical category of the verb, indicating the temporal point of view from which an event, or state of affairs, is perceived as taking place. In English, two contrasts of aspect are usually recognized. (a) The **progressive** aspect, for example *is working*, indicates that the event/state is in progress – that is, is seen from a continuing, ongoing point of view. (b) The **perfect** (sometimes called perfective) **aspect**, for example *has worked*, indicates that the event/state is seen from a completed, retrospective point of view. Both aspect constructions may be combined, as in *has been working* (called perfect progressive). There are therefore these four aspectual possibilities in English:

|  | non-progressive | progressive |
|---|---|---|
| non-perfect | *works* | *is working* |
| perfect | *has worked* | *has been working* |

The perfect construction is sometimes regarded not as an aspect, but as a **tense** form. (See **perfect; progressive.** Compare **tense.**)

assertive  see **non-assertive**

asyndetic  see **asyndeton**

**asyndeton** (adjective: **asyndetic**)   A grand word for a simple idea: it signifies the omission of connectives. Asyndeton applies particularly to the habit of omitting *and*, *or* or *but*. Alongside the normal coordination constructions:

> *men, women **and** children*
> *I'm not afraid, **but** you are.*
> *His speeches were long, boring **and** full of platitudes.*

here are asyndetic constructions:

> *men, women, children*
> *I'm not afraid – you are.*
> *His speeches were long, boring, full of platitudes.*

**attributive adjective**   An **adjective** that modifies a **noun,** for example *a **friendly** neighbour, **strange** events*. Some adjectives (for example *mere, major, utter*) are attributive only: we can say *an utter failure*, but not *\*the failure was utter*. On the other hand, some adjectives cannot be used as attributive adjectives: we can say *The rabbit was afraid*, but not *\*the afraid rabbit*. (See **adjective.**) Compare **predicative adjective**.

**auxiliary verb**   A 'helping' verb that cannot occur without a following main verb (except in cases of ellipsis). The primary verbs *be, have* and *do* are used as auxiliary verbs, but can also be used as **main verbs**. As auxiliaries, they are followed by non-finite forms of the verb, as in:

| | |
|---|---|
| *is helped* | (**passive**) |
| *is helping* | (**progressive**) |
| *has helped* | (**perfect**) |
| *does not complain* | (**dummy operator**) |

The other auxiliary verbs are known as **modal auxiliaries** (*can, must* and so on). Their main function is to express modal notions such as 'possibility', 'necessity', 'permission', and 'prediction'.

In their form, the verbs which function as auxiliaries are highly irregular:

*Be* has eight forms: *am, is, are, was, were, be, being, been*.
*Have* has four forms: *has, have, had, having*.
*Do* has five forms: *does, do, did, done, doing* (but *done* and *doing* are not used as auxiliary forms).

The modals have only one or two forms, for example *can, could*.
   Auxiliary verbs can be combined, as in **may have** *found*, **has been** *taken*, **is being** *performed*. For the patterns of combination, see **verb phrase**[1].

---

### B

**bare infinitive**   This term is used for the **base form** of the verb (for example, *be, have, take, deceive*) when used as a **non-finite** form, as in *I saw her* **open** *the safe. We'll let you* **know** *tomorrow. What we'll have to do is* **keep** *an eye on it.* The most common position of the bare infinitive is following a **modal auxiliary** or the auxiliary *do*: *You should* **eat** *something. They didn't* **see** *us.* The bare infinitive contrasts with the *to*-infinitive (the infinitive preceded by *to*), as in *What we did next was* **to telephone** *the police.* (See **infinitive**.)

**base form**   The uninflected form of the verb (or sometimes of a noun or an adjective), meaning the form which has no suffix and which is also the primary form used for representing the verb when it is put in a dictionary, for example *answer, eat, finish, make*. The base forms of the primary auxiliary verbs are *be, have* and *do*. (See **infinitive**. The base form of the English verb is also used in the **imperative**, **present tense**, and **subjunctive**.) It is also called the 'plain' form.

---

### C

**canonical**   A canonical form is the simple and typical form of a grammatical category in terms of which other more complex and atypical forms can be described. For example, a simple affirmative sentence is canonical and can be used as a basis for describing how to form negative, interrogative, imperative and exclamative sentences:

| CANONICAL | NON-CANONICAL |
|---|---|
| *They hired a bus.* | *They didn't hire a bus. Did they hire a bus?* |
| | *Hire a bus. What a bus they hired!* |

**cardinal number/numeral**    Cardinal numbers are numbers such as *one, two, three, . . . twenty-four, . . . one hundred and sixty-five*. Cardinal numbers can be spelled out, like this, or can be written in digits, as in *1, 2, 3, . . . 24, . . . 165*, and so on. Cardinal numbers are the words we use in specifying quantities, for example in answer to the question *How many . . . ?* They are distinguished from **ordinal** numbers, which specify the order of items in a list: *first, second, third, fourth* and so on. (See **numerals**.)

**case**    The grammatical term case refers to systematic variation in the form of a **noun** or **pronoun** according to its role in the syntax of the sentence. Case (**nominative, accusative, genitive**, dative, and so on) is important in many modern and classical European languages but, historically, English has lost most of its case distinctions. The only relics of the English case system today are the nominative and accusative forms of pronouns (*I ~ me*; *we ~ us*) and the **genitive** forms of nouns and pronouns (*boy's, my, ours* and so on), also called the **possessive** forms. Even these forms have lost some of their 'case' function in modern English (see **genitive**). See also **objective (case); subjective (case)**.

**catenative verb**    A verb which takes a non-finite clause as its **complement** [2], like *want* in *I want to invite you*, or *love* in *We love playing scrabble*. The term catenative (from Latin 'catena', a chain) alludes to the possibility of a recursive chain of such verbs, since the verb in the complement of the previous catenative verb can itself be a catenative verb with a non-finite complement, and so on indefinitely. A possible but rather improbable chain structure of this kind is:

Someone will need to try getting him to help mend the dishwasher.

**cause or reason, causative**    Adverbials of cause or reason express a link of cause and effect between two ideas, as in clauses introduced by *because*, *as* or *since*: *I was sick **because I ate too much trifle**.* Prepositional phrases of cause or reason are introduced by such prepositions as *because of*, *on account of*: *He couldn't see her face **because of the thick white veil**.* The same basic notion can be conveyed by causative verbs such as *angered* in *My refusal angered her*. Other examples of causative verbs are *weaken*, *beautify*, *immunize* (derived from the adjectives *weak*, *beautiful*, *immune*).

**clause**    A major unit of grammar, defined formally by the elements it may contain: **subject** (S), **verb phrase** (V), **object** (O), **complement** (C) and **adverbial** (A). All five elements of the clause are illustrated in:

| S | A | V | O | C |
|---|---|---|---|---|
| We | always | found | the teachers | very helpful. |

The verb phrase is the most central and crucial element of a clause, so it is helpful to identify a clause by first identifying its main verb. As the above example shows, a clause can be capable of standing alone as a complete **sentence**. Such clauses, called **independent** clauses, are distinct from **dependent clauses**, which generally cannot stand alone as a complete sentence and are marked by a signal or marker (for example a conjunction such as *if*) showing their subordinate status. An example of a dependent clause is:

| conjunction | S | V | O | A |
|---|---|---|---|---|
| *because* | *no one* | *has seen* | *Mars* | *at close quarters.* |

Clauses are classified in various ways. We can classify main clauses on the basis of their communicative function, as **declarative, interrogative, imperative** or **exclamative** (see **sentence types**). We can also classify dependent or **subordinate clauses** on the basis of their function within the **main clause** (as **nominal, adverbial, relative, comparative**). A third classification singles out the presence of a **finite** (or 'tensed') **verb** as crucial: on this basis, **finite clauses** are distinguished from **non-finite** clauses. For example, in contrast to *Her uncle has given her a book* (where *has* is a finite verb), the following are non-finite clauses: *having given her a book* and *to give her a book*. A further type of clause is a **verbless** clause, apparently a contradiction in terms, lacking not just the finite verb but the whole verb phrase, for example *Whatever the reason* in **Whatever the reason,** *she's less friendly than she was*. This clearly lacks the verb *be* which would be necessary to make its meaning clear: *Whatever the reason may be*. Non-finite and verbless clauses are dependent clauses, and cannot stand alone as a sentence except in unusual cases, for example in headings and captions: *How to make the headlines. Having the time of your life.* (See **finite clause**; **independent and dependent clauses**; **main clause**; **non-finite clause**; **subordinate clause**.)

**clause pattern**   see **verb pattern**

**clause type**   The terms **declarative, interrogative, imperative** and **exclamative** refer to major clause types. See also **sentence type**.

**cleft construction** (also called 'cleft clause' or 'cleft sentence')   A clause or sentence divided into two segments (hence its name 'cleft') as follows:

FIRST SEGMENT:     *It + be +* complement[1].
SECOND SEGMENT:     *that/who/which/*zero + relative clause.

|  | FIRST SEGMENT | SECOND SEGMENT |
|---|---|---|
| Example (a) | *It was my uncle* | *who gave this book to Sue* |

The most important element of a cleft construction is the **complement**[1] (following the verb *be*), which is called the 'focus'. The second segment is similar to a **relative clause,** and consists of a relative pronoun (or zero relative pronoun) followed by the rest of a clause from which the focus has been extracted. Thus example (a) above is based on a more straightforward sentence *My uncle gave this book to Sue*. Other cleft constructions based on the same sentence would make the focus not the subject, but the object or adverbial:

(b)  *It was this book that my uncle gave to Sue.*
(c)  *It was to Sue that my uncle gave this book.*

The second segment of a cleft construction is often presented as if it were already known or presupposed to be true. Hence the cleft constructions (a)–(c), although they do not differ in basic content, 'tell the same story' in different ways, and would be appropriate to different situations.

**closed interrogative clause**    Another term for a *yes-no* **interrogative,** *yes-no* **question**

**closed word classes**    see **open and closed word classes**

**collective noun**    A noun that refers to a group, or collection, of beings, for example, *audience, class, committee, crowd, gang, herd, jury, party, team*. It is possible for singular collective nouns to be followed either by a singular or a plural verb form (see **number**):

   *The audience was delighted with the performance.*
   *The audience were delighted with the performance.*

The first of these options is normal in American English. In British English both options are found. (See **concord.**)

**command**    A speech act that directs someone to do something. A command can be expressed in varied grammatical ways but is particularly associated with an **imperative** sentence such as *Leave me alone. Get your friends an inflatable raft. Be quiet.*

**common noun**    A noun which refers to a class of entities (people, things and so on) or phenomena, for example *girl*, *tiger*, *table*, *mustard*, *pessimism*. Common nouns are distinct from **proper nouns**, which refer to an individual entity (for example, *Delhi*, *Barbara*, *Microsoft*) or to a unique set of entities (for example, [*the*] *Rockies*, [*the*] *Bahamas*). Unlike proper nouns, common nouns are normally written without an initial capital letter. Common nouns make up a very large category, including most **count nouns** and all **non-count nouns**. Other categories largely included in that of common nouns are: **collective nouns, concrete nouns** and **abstract nouns**. All common nouns can be preceded by *the* (the definite article). (See **noun**.)

**comparative**    The form of a gradable word which ends (according to the regular rule) in *-er*, and which indicates a comparison of two things in terms of a higher or lower position on some scale of quality or quantity, for example *wider, colder, happier*. There are a few irregular comparative forms, for example *good ~ better, bad ~ worse, little ~ less, many/much ~ more, far ~ further*. Regular one-syllable gradable adjectives and adverbs form their comparative by adding *-(e)r*, but for most adjectives and adverbs of more than one syllable it is necessary to add the preceding adverb *more* (or *less* for a comparison in the opposite direction), for example *more careful, more slowly, less natural*. The comparative forms make a series with the **base** (uninflected) forms and **superlative** forms. See Table 1.

**comparative clause**    A subordinate clause which modifies a gradable word (adjective, adverb or determiner), and specifies the standard against which a comparison is being made. For example:

(a)  The present mayor seems more popular [*than the last one was*].

*Table 1* Comparison of adjectives, adverbs and determiners

| Examples with *-er* comparatives | | | Examples with other comparatives | | |
|---|---|---|---|---|---|
| base | comparative | superlative | base | comparative | superlative |
| *old* | *older* | *oldest* | *many* | *more* | *most* |
| *thin* | *thinner* | *thinnest* | *little* | *less* | *least* |
| *large* | *larger* | *largest* | *good* | *better* | *best* |
| *busy* | *busier* | *busiest* | *bad* | *worse* | *worst* |
| *long* | *longer* | *longest* | *modern* | *more modern* | *most modern* |
| *simple* | *simpler* | *simplest* | *important* | *more important* | *most important* |

(b)  Many people spend more money on dog food [*than they give to the church*].

(c)  It's a less valuable painting [*than I thought*].

(d)  I drove the car as fast [*as I could drive it with safety*].

Of these four sentences, (a)–(c) illustrate 'unequal comparison' (using the conjunction *than*), and (d) illustrates 'equal comparison' (using the conjunction *as*). Clauses of unequal comparison come after a comparative expression such as *older*, *more quickly*, *less popular* (see **comparative**). Clauses of equal comparison come after *as* followed by the base form of a gradable word (for example, *as big*, *as famous*, *as many*). Comparative clauses commonly contain **ellipsis**. For example, in the sentence *I drove the car as fast as I could*, the words 'drive it' are understood to be omitted at the end.

**comparative phrase**   A prepositional phrase introduced by *as* or *than* and equivalent to a comparative clause from which the verb has been omitted by ellipsis. For example, in place of (a) under comparative clause above, we can say simply [*than the last one*]. Here we may consider *than* to be a preposition, since it is followed solely by a noun phrase. Similarly: *Joan plays as well* [*as me*]. In informal English, objective pronouns such as *me* are used after *as* and *than*, even though they function in meaning as the subject of a verb (for example *play* in the example above).

The ellipsis of the verb makes it reasonable to treat the construction *as/than* + **noun phrase** as equivalent to a **prepositional phrase**.

**comparison**   see **comparative; comparative clause**. See Table 1 above for the comparison of adjectives.

**complement**   This is an ambiguous grammatical term, but the basic idea of a complement is that it is added to another constituent in order to 'complete' the meaning or structure associated with that constituent. Two definitions follow.

(1) An element of a clause which typically follows the verb *be* and which consists either of an **adjective (phrase)** or a **noun phrase**: *His ideas are **crazy**. The party had been **extremely enjoyable**. William is **the chief steward**.* Other **copular** verbs can be used instead of *be*: *Everyone felt **tired**. The wedding seemed a **quiet affair**.* This type of complement is called a **subject complement,** because it describes what the **subject** refers to (*His ideas, The party, William*). Other complements are called **object complements** because they follow the **object** and describe what the object refers to: *We found the party **extremely enjoyable**. They've made him **chief steward**.*

(2) A construction (such as a phrase or a clause) which occurs with another constituent (typically a single word) and can be said to complete the meaning or structure of that element. For example, in *We believe **that he ran that way**, I'm very fond **of spiders*** and *We've been given permission **to wear them***, the constructions in bold are complements of the words preceding them: the verb *believe*, the adjective *fond* and the noun *permission*.

Complements can be obligatory or optional. For example, *\*He deceived* is incomplete unless an object is added: *He deceived his parents.* For a verb like *deceive*, an object is an obligatory complement. But in a case like *We've been given permission to wear them*, even if the infinitive complement *to wear them* is omitted, the sentence is still acceptable: *We've been given permission.* So this complement is optional. However, when the complement of *permission* is omitted, the infinitive construction 'to do something' is still semantically implied. See **prepositional complement; verb pattern.**

**complement clause**    A clause which acts as the **complement**[2] of a word (such as a verb, an adjective or a noun) can be called a **complement clause.** Complement clauses can be *that*-**clauses,** *wh*-**clauses,** *ing*-**clauses** or **infinitive clauses.** The most common type is a complement clause following a verb, as in *I'd like to carry on* where the infinitive clause *to carry on* is the complement[2] of the verb *like.* In versions of grammar that use the concept of complement clause, it largely or entirely replaces the concept of **nominal clause** (or noun clause) referring to a clause that can occur in positions where **noun phrases** occur. For example, in *I'd like to carry on*, the infinitive complement clause is the **object** of the main clause, filling a position where a noun phrase could occur.

**complementation**    Means the same as **complement**[2]. See **verb pattern.**

**complementizer**    A word that introduces a **complement clause.** The best example of a complementizer in English is the word *that* introducing a *that*-clause as complement, as in *I believe **that God exists**.* In other versions of grammar, this *that* is called a **subordinating conjunction.**

**complex conjunction/preposition**    A conjunction or preposition consisting of more than one (written) word, for example *in order that, so long as* are complex **conjunctions;** *instead of, up to, with reference to* are complex **prepositions.**

**complex sentence**    A sentence which has one or more subordinate clauses. Compare **compound sentence.**

**compound**    A word which contains two or more other words, for example *goldfish* (consisting of *gold + fish*), *left-handed* (consisting of *left + hand + -ed*), and *gas cooker* (consisting of *gas + cooker*). We cannot rely on punctuation (for example, the use of a hyphen) to identify a compound. What makes a compound a compound is rather the ability of its parts to 'stick together' as a single word for purposes of pronunciation, grammatical behaviour and meaning. In English, there is a particular tendency for two nouns to combine together into a single compound noun (for example, *air+port*, *security+officer*). Moreover, there is a further tendency for such compounds to combine with other nouns or compounds into still larger combinations, for example *airport security officer*, *real estate tax shelter sales people*.

**compound sentence**    A sentence which contains two or more clauses linked by **coordination,** for example *We went to meet her at the airport, but the plane was delayed.* Compare **complex sentence.**

**concessive adverbial, concessive clause**    An adverbial clause or other adverbial which expresses a contrast of meaning or implication of 'unexpectedness' in its relation to the matrix clause of the sentence of which it is part. Concessive clauses are introduced by such concessive conjunctions as *although* and *though*: [*Although the car was badly damaged*], *none of the passengers was hurt.* Concessive phrases are introduced by such prepositions as **despite** and **in spite of**: *We enjoyed our holiday* [*in spite of the weather*]. (See **adverbial; adverbial clause.**)

**concessive conjunction**    see **concessive adverbial**

**concord** (also called **agreement**)    In the most general terms, concord is a relation between two elements such that they match one another in terms of some grammatical feature. In English, the most important type of concord is number concord between **subject** and (**finite**) **verb**. This means that a singular subject is followed by a singular verb (for example, *My brother owns a* *yacht*), and a plural subject is followed by a plural verb (for example, *My brothers own a yacht*). A breach of concord (as in \**My brother own a yacht*) is ungrammatical in standard English. However, there are frequent exceptions to this general rule, and explanations of many of them make use of the concept of notional concord – the idea that the subject and verb can agree in terms of their meaning, rather than strictly in terms of form. For example, the use of a plural verb after a **collective noun** such as *crowd* or after the **indefinite pronoun** *none* can be explained if we consider that the subjects in (a) and (b) involve more than one person:

(a)   The jury have come to their decision.
(b)   None of the guests take sugar in their tea.

In addition to subject-verb concord, there is also noun-pronoun concord, that is agreement between a pronoun and its **antecedent** in terms of number, person, and gender (for example, *Mary . . . she . . .; James . . . he . . .; the house . . . it . . .*). This, again, is influenced by 'notional concord', as we see from the use of the plural *their* in examples (a) and (b) above. (See **negative concord**.)

**concrete noun**    A noun referring to physical phenomena, whether persons, animals, things or substances, for example *student*, *rabbit*, *bus*, *grease*. Concrete nouns are the opposite of **abstract nouns**.

**conditional clause**    An **adverbial clause** expressing a condition. Most conditional clauses begin with the conjunction *if* (*if*-clauses). Another conditional conjunction, with negative meaning, is *unless*. Other conditional conjunctions are *so long as*, *as long as*, *provided that* and *on condition that*:

(a)   [*If you take this medicine*], you will feel better.
(b)   Emotions are dangerous [*unless they are controlled*].
(c)   You can stay here [*provided that you look after yourselves*].

When the verb is in the hypothetical **past tense**, conditional clauses express 'unreal' meaning:

(d)  [*If she **knew** about his behaviour*], she would never forgive him.

(e)  I would have invited you [*if I **had realized** you were in town*].

(To express an 'unreal' meaning in the main clause, *would* is used.) Sentence (e) illustrates the hypothetical **past perfect**, referring to an unreal, or imaginary, happening in the past.

In teaching English grammar, the sentence types illustrated by examples (a), (d) and (e) are called 'first conditional', 'second conditional' and 'third conditional'. But the most common type of conditional sentence is the one illustrated by (b), with a present tense verb in both clauses. (See **hypothetical past; past tense; subjunctive**.)

**conditional conjunctions**    The words *if* and *unless* are examples of conditional conjunctions. See **conditional clause**.

**conditional tense**    A term sometimes used for the **hypothetical past** or the *were*-subjunctive.

**conjunct**    (1) Another term for a **linking adverbial** (for example, *however, therefore, moreover*).

(2) One of the constituents of a coordinate construction. For example, in the coordinate noun phrase *money brokers and estate agents*, *money brokers* and *estate agents* are two conjuncts linked by *and*.

**conjunction**    A term which refers generally to words that have a conjoining or linking role in grammar. In practice, 'conjunction' refers to two rather different classes of words: **coordinating conjunctions** (*and, or, but* and sometimes *nor*) and **subordinating conjunctions** (*if, when, because* and so on). These are sometimes called 'coordinators' and 'subordinators' respectively. The coordinators are used to coordinate, or link, two or more units of the same status (for example, two main clauses or two noun phrases). The subordinators, on the other hand, are placed at the beginning of a **subordinate clause** to link it into the main clause. (See **coordination; subordinate clause; subordination.**)

**constituent**    A grammatically defined part of a larger unit of grammatical structure. For example, all the words and phrases that make up a clause are constituents of that clause.

**construction**    A grammatical way of combining parts of a sentence into larger groupings. For example, the 'progressive construction' combines a form of the verb *be* with the *-ing* form of a second verb.

**content clause**    In the framework of *The Cambridge Grammar of the English Language*, a content clause is a very general category of subordinate clause, which lacks the distinguishing features of **relative clauses** and **comparative clauses**. The content clause concept makes the categories of **adverbial clause** and **nominal clause** unnecessary in this framework.

**continuous**    A term used instead of **progressive** in many pedagogical treatments of English grammar. 'The present continuous' is used instead of 'the present progressive', and so on. (See **progressive.**)

**contracted form, contraction**    A reduced or shortened form of a word. For example, the negative word *not* is frequently contracted to *n't* in speech (for example, *isn't, wasn't, couldn't*). The auxiliary verbs *be, have, will* and *would*, and the main verb *be*, are frequently contracted as follows:

| | | | |
|---|---|---|---|
| contractions of *be*: | *am* ~ *'m* | *is* ~ *'s* | *are* ~ *'re* |
| contractions of *have*: | *have* ~ *'ve* | *has* ~ *'s* | *had* ~ *'d* |
| contractions of *will* and *would*: | | *will* ~ *'ll* | *would* ~ *'d* |

For example: *I'm tired. She's arrived. They're here. We've finished. John's left. It'll be all right.*

**contrast, clause of**    see **concessive clause**

**conversion**    The derivational process of converting a word from one word class to another. For example, ***text*** is primarily a noun, but it can nowadays be used as a verb *text*, *texting* and so on, in the context of text messaging.

**coordinate clause**    see **compound sentence; coordination**

**coordinating conjunction, coordinator**    One of the words *and*, *or*, *but* and (sometimes) *nor*. See **conjunction; coordination.**

**coordination**    The joining of two or more constituents of equivalent status, normally by the use of a coordinating conjunction (*and*, *or*, *but* or *nor*), so as to form a larger grammatical unit having the function that each of its parts would have on their own. For example:

(a)   She wore [$^1$[$^2$a leather coat$^2$] and [$^3$fur-lined boots$^3$]$^1$].

In (a), the two noun phrases *a leather coat* and *fur-lined boots* are coordinated in order to form a larger one, *a leather coat and fur-lined boots*. All three of the constituents (1, 2 and 3) are of the same basic kind. Coordination can take place at different levels of syntax: example (a) shows coordination between **phrases**; (b) shows coordination between **clauses**; and (c) shows coordination between words:

(b)   [[These photographs are yours], but [those are mine]].
(c)   The children who come [[first], [second] and [third]] will each win a prize.

These examples illustrate the basic pattern of coordination, but there are many variations of this pattern (see particularly **asyndeton; correlative**). Coordination and **subordination** are often thought of as complementary, but in fact they are very different ways of elaborating the structure of a sentence.

**copula**    The verb *be* when used as a main verb. (Copula is also sometimes used for other **copular verbs**.)

**copular verb** (also called copulative or linking verb)    A main verb which, like the verb *be*, links or 'couples' a subject to a subject complement[1]. *Be* is by far the most common copular verb and is called the **copula**:

> Those cakes *are* delicious.
> The meeting *was* a great success.

Other copular verbs add an extra meaning to the neutral meaning of *be*:

> Those cakes *look* delicious.
> The meeting *proved* a great success.

Some other verbs that can act as copular verbs are: *sound, feel, smell, taste, appear, seem, become, get, go, grow, turn*. Note that *be* and some other copular verbs can also be followed by an adverbial:

> The meeting will be *at five o'clock*.
> Everyone will be *there*.

**corefer (to), coreference, coreferential**    These three terms (verb, noun and adjective) denote the important mechanism, in grammar, whereby one expression refers to the same thing, person and so on as another expression in the same sentence. Among the vehicles of coreference in English are (a) **personal**, (b) **reflexive** and (c) **relative pronouns**:

(a)    *Margery* was asking if *she* could come.
(b)    *People* express *themselves* in different ways.
(c)    No, that was *Yoko*, *who* was teaching with me.

The words in italics in these examples are coreferential. In (a), however, there is another interpretation: *she* could refer to some other female person, mentioned earlier in the discourse.

**correlative**    A term used of a construction in which two parts of a sentence are linked together by two words – one word belonging to one part and the other word belonging to the other. An instance of correlative **coordination** is: *The battle took place* [*both on the sea and on land*]. Two prepositional phrases are here conjoined by placing *both* in front of one constituent and *and* in front of the other. The use of correlative words adds emphasis and clarity to the construction. Other correlative co-ordinators are *either . . . or . . .*, *neither . . . nor . . .*, and *not only . . . but . . . .*

**Subordination**, as well as coordination, can be correlative: *If the car is too old for repair, **then** it will have to be scrapped.* Here the adverb *then* in the main clause reinforces the conditional meaning of *if* in the subordinate clause (see **conditional clause**).

**count noun** (also called **countable noun**)    A **noun** which has both a singular and a plural form (for example, *picture ~ pictures*, *child ~ children*, *attack ~ attacks*). Count nouns can be preceded by the **indefinite article** *a/an* (for example, *a child*, *an attack*) or, in the plural, by words such as *many*, *few*, *these* or the **cardinal numbers** 2, 3, 4, . . . (for example, *many pictures*, *these children*, *three attacks*). (Note that words like *sheep* and *deer*, which are unchanged in the plural, are nevertheless count nouns, because they combine with such 'counting words' as in *many/three/these sheep*.) Count nouns contrast with **non-count** nouns, which do not have a plural and do not combine with these 'counting words', for example *blood*, *silver*, *money*, *furniture*, *infor-mation*, *advice*. Many nouns, however, can be either count or non-count, depending on their meaning and context. For example, *glass* is non-count when referring to the transparent substance, but count when referring to glass vessels or spectacles: *How much glass do you need?* (that is 'to glaze these windows') contrasts with *How many glasses do you need?* (that is for drinks at a party). Many words which are principally count nouns can exceptionally be used as non-count nouns and vice versa. (For example, *food* is generally non-count, but when talking of *baby foods* or *pet foods*, we use it as a count noun.) (See **non-count noun; noun; plural.**)

---

### D

**declarative clause**   A **clause** which expresses a statement or proposition, normally making some assertion about the universe of reality, for example: *I've broken my watch. Pluto is invisible to the naked eye.* In a declarative clause normally the **subject** precedes the **verb** phrase, which in turn precedes other elements such as **object** and **complement**[1]. See **clause, sentence types.**

**defining relative clause**   Another name for restrictive relative clauses. (See **restrictive and non-restrictive relative clauses.**)

**definite article**   The word *the*, the most common word in English. *The* is a **determiner** and normally introduces a **noun phrase**. Its function is to indicate that the noun phrase refers to something which is uniquely identifiable in the shared knowledge of the speaker and hearer. For example, by saying *on the ship*, a speaker implies that hearers can work out which ship is meant. Contrast this with the use of the **indefinite article** (for example, *a ship*). (See **articles; generic.**)

**degree adverb/adverbial**   An adverb(ial) which indicates the degree or extent to which some quality or quantity applies to the situation described, for example *very quickly*; *utterly useless*; *He loves her to distraction*. Degree adverb(ial)s normally modify gradable words, especially gradable adjectives, adverbs and verbs. (See **adverb; adverbial; gradable word.**)

**deictic** (abstract noun: **deixis**)   A word which points to, or indicates, what it refers to is termed deictic. Common deictic words are the demonstratives *this*, *that*, *these* and *those*; the place adverbs *here* and *there*; and the time adverbs *now* and *then*. Deictics shift their reference according to the context in which they are used. For example, the meaning of *I'll meet you there this evening* is not clear, unless we know from the context (either from what has been said, or from the situation outside language) which place is meant by *there* and which evening is meant by *this evening*. 'Deixis' is the noun corresponding to the adjective 'deictic'. (See **demonstrative**.)

**demonstrative**   The four words *this*, *that*, *these* and *those* are called demonstratives. When they are followed by some other word (especially a noun) in a noun phrase, they are demonstrative **determiners**: *this machine*; *that old bicycle*; *these people*; *those bizarre incongruities that life occasionally throws up*. When they act as the **head** (and typically the only word) of a noun phrase, they are demonstrative **pronouns**: *This is a fascinating programme. Whose gloves are those?* The demonstratives are so called because they have the function of 'showing' or 'pointing to' something in the context. They are **deictic** words. Of the four demonstratives, *this* and *that* are singular, while *these* and *those* are plural. In very general terms, *this* and *these* have 'immediate' or 'nearby' reference, while *that* and *those* have 'non-immediate' or 'more distant' reference. (Note that *that* is not always a demonstrative: it can also be a **conjunction** or a **relative pronoun**. See *that*-**clause**.)

**demonstrative pronoun**    see **demonstrative**

**dependent**   Used as a noun, the word **dependent** refers to a element that combines in construction with the **head** of a phrase. Dependents are either **complements**[(2)], which are closely bound to the head, or **modifiers**, which are more loosely linked to the head as optional elements.

**dependent clause**   A **clause** which is dependent on (that is, included in the structure of) another clause. (See **independent and dependent clauses**. See also the similar concept of **subordinate clause**.)

**derivational morphology**    see **morphology**

**determiner** (also called **determinative**)    A word which 'determines' or 'specifies' how the reference of a noun phrase is to be understood. For example, *this* determines the reference of *table* in *this table*: it tells us which or what table is intended. Determiners normally precede a **noun**, and indeed precede all other words in a **noun phrase**: *this old table you bought*; *some other people*; *what a strange sight*. The **articles** *the* and *a/an* are the most common determiners. Other determiners are the **demonstrative** determiners *this*, *that*, *these* and *those*; **possessive** determiners (or pronouns) *my*, *you*, *their* and so on; **indefinite** determiners such as *all*, *some*, *much*, *each*; *wh*-**word** determiners such as *which*, *what* and *whose*. In position, some determiners can precede others: *all* (known as a predeterminer) precedes *the* in *all the dishes*; *the* precedes *many* (known as a postdeterminer) in *the many meetings I have attended*. Words like *the*, *this* and *my* are known as central determiners. The determiners are an example of a closed class of function words. In an older tradition of grammar, determiners were treated as adjectives, and terms like 'demonstrative adjective' and 'possessive adjective' are still used in some grammars (See **function words**; **word-class**.)

**direct object**    An object which follows the verb phrase and which typically indicates the person, thing and so on directly affected by the main verb's meaning. In *Many animals rear **their young** in burrows*, *their young* is the object. Direct objects are contrasted with **indirect objects**: in *I've sent Maggie a thank-you letter*, *Maggie* is the indirect object and *a thank-you letter* is the direct object. (For further details, see **object**.)

**direct question**    see **question**

**direct speech**   A mode of reporting what someone has said, in which we reproduce the actual words spoken or written. In narrative, direct speech is normally signalled by being enclosed in quotation marks: in *'Look after yourself,' said Jonah*, *'Look after yourself'* is in direct speech. Direct speech contrasts with indirect or reported speech: *Jonah told me **to look after myself**.* (See **reported speech**.)

**discontinuous construction**   A phrase or other construction divided into two (or more) segments which are separated by words not part of the phrase is called discontinuous. For example, in *A time will come when the world will regret this decision*, the predicate *will come* separates the first part of the subject noun phrase (*A time . . .*) from the rest (*. . . when the world . . .*). The discontinuity could be avoided if *will come* were moved to the end of the sentence: *A time when . . . decision will come*. However, discontinuity is sometimes desirable, as it avoids an unbalanced sentence. (See **end weight**.)

**disjunct**   see **sentence adverbial**

**ditransitive verb**   A **verb** which takes two **objects** in its **verb pattern**: for example, ***lend*** in *I should have lent you my keys*. In this sentence, *you* is described as the **indirect object** and *my keys* as the **direct object**.

**double negative**   see **negative concord**

**dummy, dummy word**   A word which fills a grammatical position but is 'empty' of meaning. For example, the verb *do*, used as an **auxiliary**, is often called the dummy operator because it has no meaning of its own but exists simply to fill the 'slot' of **operator** when an operator is needed to form (for example) negative or interrogative sentences. In a similar way, *it* can be called a **dummy subject** when it fills the subject slot in sentences like: *It's a pity that they wasted so much time*. Compare with *That they* *wasted so much time is a pity*. (See **extraposition**; **introductory** *it*; **operator**.)

**dummy operator**    see **auxiliary verb**; **dummy**; **negation**; **operator**; **past simple**

**dummy subject**    see **dummy**; **existential there**

**duration adverb/adverbial**    An **adverb(ial)** specifying length of time, for example: *The hostages have not been seen **for several years**. I waited **all night** for a phone call*. (See **adverb**; **adverbial**.)

---

### E

**echo question**    A question which repeats a previous utterance and amounts to a request for the repetition of that utterance (or at least of part of it). We use echo questions either because we did not fully hear or understand what was said, or because its content is too surprising to be believed. For example:

| (It cost £5,000.) | HOW much did it cost? |
| (His son's an osteopath.) | His son's a WHAT? |

Echo questions are usually spoken with a rising intonation, and with a strong emphasis on the *wh*-word (*what*, *who*, *how* and so on). (See **question**; *wh*-**question**.)

**-ed clause**    (also called a past participle construction)    A **subordinate non-finite** clause in which the main verb (and only verb word) is an *-ed* form. For example:

(a)  A man was killed by two shots from a thirty-eight calibre revolver *fired at close range*.
(b)  *Refused entry to the country*, we had to return home immediately.

Some *-ed* clauses, like (a), modify nouns and are similar to **relative clauses**. Other *-ed* clauses, like (b), are **adverbial**. Generally speaking, an *-ed* clause is like a **passive** clause, but has no **subject** or **finite verb**. (The implied subject is the head of the noun phrase, like *revolver* in (a), or the subject of the main clause, like *we* in (b).) But sometimes an adverbial *-ed* clause does have a subject, for example *All things considered, the meeting was a success.* (See *-ed* **form; non-finite clause**.)

**-ed form, -ed participle**    The **past participle** form of a verb, used to form the **perfect** after *have* (for example, *has changed*); to form the **passive** after *be* (for example, *are changed*); and to act as the verb in a non-finite *-ed* **clause** (for example, *Convinced of his innocence, the Queen ordered his release*). The *-ed* form of regular verbs ends in *-ed* (for example, *looked, prepared, tied*). The *-ed* form of **irregular verbs** takes many different forms (for example, *blown, sung, sent*), some ending in *-en* (for example, *been, taken, eaten*). With regular verbs and many irregular verbs, the *-ed* participle is identical to the **past tense** form.

**ellipsis**    The grammatically allowed omission of one or more words from a sentence, where the words omitted can be precisely reconstructed. For example (^ shows the point at which ellipsis occurs):

(a)  That car is older than this ^.
(b)  Have you seen Samantha? No, I haven't ^.
(c)  Most children have travelled more widely than their parents ^.
(d)  Boys will be boys, and girls ^ girls.

These examples show (a) ellipsis of a **noun,** (b) ellipsis of a **predication,** (c) ellipsis of a **predicate** and (d) ellipsis of a **verb phrase.** Usually, as in these examples, the words omitted can be reconstructed because the same words occur in the context. For example, in (a) the ellipsis avoids the repetition of the word *car*. In avoiding repetition, ellipsis is similar in its function to **substitution** (for example, the use of pro-forms such as *one* and *do so*), and is sometimes referred to as 'substitution by **zero**'.

**embedding** (or **nesting**)   The inclusion of one unit as part of another unit of the same general type. For example, embedding of one phrase inside another is very common. In [*at* [*the other end* [*of* [*the road*]]]], one **prepositional phrase** [*of the road*] is embedded in another [*at the other end of the road*]; also, one **noun phrase** [*the road*] is embedded in another noun phrase [*the other end of the road*]. Another major type of embedding is that of subordination of clauses – the inclusion of one clause (a **subordinate clause**) inside another one (the **main clause**). Embedding is one of the two devices of grammar that enable us to construct sentences which are as complex as we want – the other device being coordination.

**emphasis**   A word referring generally to prominence given to one part of an utterance rather than another, for example by the use of stress, intonation or particular words. In grammar, the term 'emphasis' has no precise meaning. However, we can note a number of emphatic grammatical devices, such as word order (see **end focus**), **cleft constructions**, the emphatic use of *do* (see **operator**), the emphatic use of reflexive pronouns (for example, *the President himself*) (see **reflexive pronoun**) and the use of **degree adverbs** such as *so* and *absolutely* (for example, *it's so/absolutely unfair!*) (see **intensification**). Emotive emphasis can be conveyed also by **interjections** and **exclamations**.

**end focus**   The principle by which elements placed towards the end of a phrase, clause or sentence tend to receive the focus or prominence associated with new information (see **given and new information**). Compare:

(a)   I'm giving Rosie this dress.
(b)   I'm giving this dress to Rosie.

Sentences (a) and (b) suggest different situations: in (a) 'this dress' is new information – the speaker may be showing the dress to a friend for the first time; in (b) 'to Rosie' is new information – the hearer may be looking at the dress already, but Rosie is now being mentioned, for the first time, as its recipient. Thus, in both cases, there is a tendency to put new information in a position of prominence at the end.

End focus is important to grammar, because it helps to explain why, where grammar offers a choice of different word orders, we choose one order rather than another. An example is the choice between **active** and **passive**. In spoken language, end focus tends to coincide with intonational emphasis. Compare **end weight**.

**end weight**    In grammar, end weight is the principle by which longer and more complex units tend to occur later in the sentence than shorter and less complex units. For example, in sentences consisting of subject, verb phrase and object, the subject is likely to be short and simple in comparison with the object. Where English grammar allows a choice of different word orders, end weight helps to explain the choice of one order rather than another. For example, we can vary the order of the particle and object in a **phrasal verb** construction such as *put* (something) *off*. When the object is a personal pronoun, the order object + particle is always preferred, as in *They put it off*. If the object is a longer noun phrase, for example the meeting, then both orders can be used:

We'll have to *put* the meeting *off* ~ We'll have to *put off* the meeting.

When the object is even longer and more complex, the position object + particle becomes increasingly unacceptable because of an increasing violation of the end weight principle:

(a)  We'll have to *put* the next meeting of the General Assembly *off*.
(b)  We'll have to *put off* the next meeting of the General Assembly.

The order of (b) is clearly much more acceptable than that of (a). End weight is closely related to **end focus**.

**exclamation** A kind of utterance which has as its major function the expression of strong feeling. Exclamations can vary from single exclamatory words such as *Oh!* (called an **interjection**) to sentences with a full clause structure, including a verb phrase, as in *It's so absurd!* English has a special **exclamative** clause or sentence structure, beginning with *what* or *how*:

(a) What a strange sight they saw!
(b) How lovely she looks!

The element containing *what* or *how* may, for example, be an **object,** as in (a), or a **subject complement,** as in (b). The rest of the main clause follows, usually in its normal statement order: for example, in (a) the order is object + subject + verb phrase; in (b) the order is complement + subject + verb phrase. The rest of the clause, after the *wh*-element, is often omitted, so that a verb-less sentence results: *What a strange sight! How lovely!* A final exclamation mark (*!*) is the typical signal of an exclamation in writing, although it has no grammatical import. (See **sentence types.**) Compare **statement; question.**

**exclamative, exclamative clause** see **clause, exclamation**

**exclamatory question** A kind of *yes-no* **question** having the force of an exclamation. Exclamatory questions are often negative in form and are spoken with falling intonation rather than with the rising intonation associated with ordinary yes-no questions: *Isn't this fun!* or (of someone else's children) *Haven't they grown!*

**exclusive *we*** see **inclusive *we***

**existential construction** A clause or simple sentence with **existential *there*** as subject.

**existential *there*** The word *there* used as a dummy **subject** at the beginning of a clause or sentence, as in:

(a)   There will be trouble.
(b)   There's nothing happening tonight.
(c)   There were too many people in the room.
(d)   There has been a lot of money wasted.

Existential *there* is so called because it introduces sentences which postulate the existence of some state of affairs. Normally the sentence has *be* as its main verb. Existential *there*, unlike *there* as an adverb of place, is unstressed. The noun phrase following *be* can be seen as a delayed subject and *there* as a dummy subject inserted to fill the vacant subject position. Compare (d), for example, with the more standard word order of: *A lot of money has been wasted*. The delayed subject is usually indefinite in meaning, and sometimes shows its subject status by determining whether the verb phrase is singular or plural (see **concord**): compare (c) above with *There was too much noise in the room*. Nevertheless, in other ways, the status of subject belongs to *there*. For example, *there* comes after the operator in questions (*Is there anything happening?*) and occurs as matching subject in **tag questions** (*There's plenty of food left, isn't there?*) Hence the question of what is the subject of an existential sentence is problematic.

**extraposition, extraposed**   Extraposition is a special construction where a **subordinate clause**, acting as **subject** of a main clause, is 'extraposed' – that is, placed at the end of the main clause – and replaced by *it* as an initial subject:

(a)   [That the expedition failed] was a pity. ~
(b)   It was a pity [that the expedition failed].

Sentence (a) illustrates the normal subject-verb order, and (b) illustrates extraposition.
    Not only a *that*-clause, but **nominal clauses** in general can be 'extraposed' in this way. For example, an **infinitive clause** is extraposed in:

(c)   It pays [to send your kids to a good school].

It is obvious that extraposition serves the purposes of **end weight** and **end focus**. Thus (c) would be an extremely awkward violation of end weight if the normal subject-first order were used: [*To send your kids to a good school*] *pays*.

---

**F**

**feminine**   In English grammar, feminine means having female, rather than male, reference (in contrast to **masculine**). Feminine and masculine forms traditionally make up the grammatical category of **gender**. In English grammar, the feminine gender is marked only in third-person singular **pronouns**: *she*, *her*, *hers* and *herself* are feminine pronouns. (Some **nouns** are also marked as having female reference, for example by the ending -*ess* in *princess*, *goddess* and *lioness*.) (See **masculine; personal pronoun**.)

**finite**   see **finite verb**

**finite clause**   A **clause** which has a **finite verb**. For example, in [*When he's working*], *he likes* [*to be left alone*], the **subordinate clause** *When he's working* is a finite clause; likewise the main clause, which has *likes* as its verb phrase. But the infinitive clause *to be left alone* is **non-finite**: it has no finite verb. (See **finite verb; non-finite clause; verb phrase**.)

**finite verb**   The forms of a verb that vary for **present tense** and **past tense** are called **finite**. Hence finite verbs are sometimes called 'tensed' verbs. Both auxiliaries and main verbs have finite forms (see Table 2).

The **base** form of a verb (such as *see*, *listen*) is finite when it is used as a present tense form, but **non-finite** when it is used as an **infinitive**. Similarly, the -*ed* **form** of regular verbs is finite when it is used as a past tense form and non-finite when it is used as an -*ed* **participle** (past participle). **Modal auxiliaries** (for example, *can*, *could*, *may*, *might*, *must*) can be considered finite verbs, even though some of them lack a past tense form.

*Table 2* Finite verb forms

| Present tense | *am, is* | *has* | *does* | *sees* | *makes* | *listens* |
|---|---|---|---|---|---|---|
| | *are* | *have* | *do* | *see* | *make* | *listen* |
| Past tense | *was, were* | *had* | *did* | *saw* | *made* | *listened* |
| (non-finite forms) | (*be, being, been*) | (*have, having, had*) | (*do, doing, done*) | (*see, seeing, seen*) | (*make, making, made*) | (*listen, listening, listened*) |

**Verb phrases** are called finite when they begin with (or consist of) a finite verb: for example, *works, is working, has worked; has been taking, was taken, was being taken* are all finite verb phrases. (See **finite clause; non-finite verb; past tense; present tense; verb phrase**.)

**first conditional**    see **conditional clause**

**first person**    see **first person pronoun; imperative; person**

**first person pronoun**    A **pronoun** referring to the speaker or writer (with or without other people). The first person singular pronouns are *I, me, my, mine,* and *myself.* The first person plural pronouns are *we, us, our, ours, ourselves.* (See **person; personal pronoun; possessive; reflexive pronoun**.)

**foreign plural**    Some **nouns** that have been borrowed into English from other languages form their plural on the pattern of the foreign (or classical) language from which they come. In other words, they have 'foreign plurals'. For example:

| | | |
|---|---|---|
| *stimulus ~ stimuli* | *stratum ~ strata* | (Latin) |
| *axis ~ axes* | *criterion ~ criteria* | (Greek) |
| *corps ~ corps* | *rendezvous ~ rendezvous* | (French) |
| *virtuoso ~ virtuosi* | *tempo ~ tempi* | (Italian) |
| *seraph ~ seraphim* | *cherub ~ cherubim* | (Hebrew) |

Often a foreign noun can be used with a **regular** plural as well as with its foreign plural. For instance, the Latin plural of *index*, *indices*, is used in technical contexts, but the regular plural of *indexes* is preferred in everyday use, for example in referring to the indexes at the back of a book. (See **irregular plurals; plural**.)

**formal and informal**    Terms used of 'higher' and 'lower' levels of style or usage in English. Formal style is associated with careful usage, especially written language, whereas informal style is associated with colloquial usage, especially spoken, conversational language in relaxed or private settings. Formal features of English grammar include the placing of **prepositions** before a *wh*-**word**, for example *To whom does the house belong?*, as contrasted with the more informal (and usual) *Who does the house belong to?* One feature of informal English grammar is the use of verb and negative **contractions**, for example *She's ill* (more formal: *She is ill*) and *couldn't* (more formal: *could not*). Formal grammar is more influenced by the tradition of Latin-based grammar: for example, the pronoun *I* is formal in **comparative** constructions such as *My brother was taller than I*, as opposed to *My brother was taller than me*. See also **functional**.

**formulaic**    A general term used to describe some piece of language whose grammatical and lexical form is more or less fixed or fossilized, so that it cannot easily be varied as normal grammatically formed expressions can. 'Formulaic' can be applied, at one extreme, to a single word, like *Thanks*; at the other extreme, to a whole sentence, like *How do you do?*. For example, this sentence cannot have its pronoun or tense or verb changed: *\*How did you do? \*How do they do? \*How do you keep?* One reason for this is that formulaic expressions can include old-fashioned or archaic grammar, such as the archaic use of the **present simple** in *How do you do* (compare the **progressive** in *How are you doing?*). The term 'formulaic' is applied to the **subjunctive** form of the verb used in formulae such as *God save the Queen* or *Long live the bride and groom*.

**frequency adverb/adverbial**     An **adverb**, **adverbial phrase** or **adverbial clause** which says how often an event takes place. For example, *rarely* in *We rarely meet nowadays* is a frequency adverb. Other examples are *always*, *usually*, *frequently*, *often*, *sometimes*, *occasionally*, *never*, *hardly ever*, *every year*, *twice a week*, *whenever I write to her*. Frequency adverbials answer the question 'How often?' or 'How many times?'

**front position**     The position of an adverbial when it occurs at the beginning of a clause, before the subject. For example, *Normally* in (a) and *At 12:50 p.m.* in (b) are in front position:

(a)  *Normally*, the train arrives on time.
(b)  *At 12:50 p.m.* a ramp was rolled up to the plane.

**function words** (or grammatical words)     Words that are defined by their role or function in grammar rather than in terms of dictionary definition. Function words (such as *of*, *if* and *and*) contrast with lexical or 'content words' such as **nouns** and **adjectives**. The main classes of function words are **determiners**, **prepositions**, **conjunctions**, **auxiliary verbs** and **pronouns**. (See also **open and closed word classes**.)

**functional**     The word functional is an ambiguous term in grammar.

(1) An approach to grammar is functional if it focuses attention on the way grammar contributes to the social uses of language and the way language is processed by the human mind.

(2) A description or definition of some part of a clause or sentence is functional if it describes it in terms of the part or role that it plays in the whole clause or sentence. For example, a functional description of a **noun phrase** says how the noun phrase behaves in a larger unit – a **clause** – of which it is a part, that is as **subject, object, prepositional complement** and so on. In contrast, a formal definition of a noun phrase looks at how it is constructed of smaller constituents – for example, nouns, determiners and various kinds of modifier.

Both 'functional'[1] and 'functional'[2] have 'formal' as their opposite term.

**fused relative construction**    Another term for a **nominal relative clause.**

**future constructions**    Grammatical word combinations used in referring to future time. In English, the modal *will* is the most common way of referring to things happening in the future, for example: *The Women's Final* **will** *take place next Saturday*. The *will* + **infinitive** construction is sometimes called the 'future tense', but it is not comparable to the **past tense** and **present tense** which are indicated by morphological forms of the verb word itself (for example, *work(s)* and *worked*, in contrast to the future construction *will work*). *Will* has its own past tense form *would*, which can indicate 'future-in-the-past', as in *Marianne was glad that her journey* **would** *soon be over*. Also, combined with the **perfect** *have* + *ed*-form, *will* can indicate 'past-in-the-future', for example *By age 20, an American child* **will have watched** *700,000 TV commercials*.

Apart from *will*, there are a number of other ways of indicating the future in English using verbs. The most common are:

| | |
|---|---|
| *be* going to – | *I***'m going to buy** *you a present.* |
| **present progressive** – | *She's* **meeting** *me tomorrow.* |
| **present simple** (especially in **subordinate clauses**) – | *Phone us when you* **arrive** *this evening.* |
| *will* + progressive – | *Next week's programme* **will be starting** *half an hour earlier.* |
| *shall* + infinitive (in formal style, with first person subjects) – | *We* **shall** *look forward to receiving your order.* |

(See **modal auxiliary; past tense; present tense.**)

**future perfect**    The verb construction consisting of a future construction + **perfect infinitive** (for example, *will have eaten*), referring to something which, from a future standpoint, is seen to have happened in the past. (See **future constructions; perfect**.)

## G

**gap**    A place in a sentence where there is no visible or audible constituent, but where a constituent seems to be needed by the structure of the sentence. For example, in *She's older than I am*, the end of the sentence has a gap, a missing complement[1] corresponding to the word *old*. Compare **zero**.

**gender**    The grammatical category which distinguishes **masculine, feminine** and **neuter** (or non-personal) pronouns. In English grammar, gender is limited to third-person singular personal and reflexive pronouns: *he, him, his* and *himself* are masculine; *she, her, hers* and *herself* are feminine; and *it, its, itself* are neuter. Gender has been a prominent issue in discussions of grammar in recent years: since English lacks a singular personal pronoun which is neutral between male and female reference, it has been felt desirable to avoid the traditional masculine bias of generic *he*, for example by using *he or she* or *they*. Compare:

(a)   Everyone thinks *he* has the answer.
(b)   Everyone thinks *he or she* has the answer.
(c)   Everyone thinks *they* have the answer.

In recent years, for 'unisex' reference, the use of (a) *he* has declined, whereas the use of (b) *he or she* and (c) *they* has increased. However, the use of *they* in examples like (c) causes controversy because it is felt to be a breach of **concord**. (See **feminine; masculine; personal pronoun**.)

**generic**    Referring to a whole class rather than to individual members of a class. For example, the subjects of (a), (b) and (c) are generic (referring to computers in general):

(a)  The computer is a remarkable machine.
(b)  A computer is a remarkable machine.
(c)  Computers are remarkable machines.

In contrast, the subjects of (d) and (e) are not generic, since they refer to an individual computer:

(d)  The computer isn't working: it needs repair.
(e)  A computer has been stolen from the laboratory.

Note that the definite and indefinite articles (*the* and *a*) are generic in some contexts and specific in others. The articles are usually specific in meaning, but when *the* comes before an adjective as head of the noun phrase, it is normally generic: *the rich*, *the unemployed, the absurd*.

**genitive**    The form of a **noun** or **noun phrase** ending in *'s* (apostrophe *s*) or *s'* (*s* apostrophe) and indicating possession or some such meaning. (Apart from a few special cases, the *s'* spelling is restricted to the genitive ending of regular plural nouns, such as *boys ~ boys'*.) The genitive form of a noun typically comes before another noun, the head of the noun phrase of which the genitive is part, for example *Robert's desk*. Historically, the genitive is the only remnant in modern English of the **case** system of nouns, prevalent in Old English, and also in classical Greek, Latin and many modern European languages. The *of*-phrase (sometimes called the '*of*-genitive') has replaced the genitive in many usages; in others, both constructions can be used, for example *the arrival of the bride = the bride's arrival*. In modern English, the genitive is strictly speaking no longer a case-ending at all: rather, it is an ending added to noun phrases, such as [*the bride's*] in [*the bride's*] *arrival* above, or [*my father's*] in [*my father's*] *favourite breakfast*. Note that *my* belongs with *father's* in this example rather than with *breakfast*.

Usually the genitive fills a **determiner** slot in the larger noun phrase of which it is part: hence the function of *the bride's* above is similar to that of *her* in *her arrival* or *the* in *the arrival*.

Potentially, the genitive may be quite a complicated phrase. But there is a tendency to prefer the *of*-construction where the genitive would cause too much complexity in front of the head noun. Hence *the night train to Edinburgh's departure* is less likely to occur than *the departure of the night train to Edinburgh*. Notice in this example, however, that the placing of the *'s* at the end of Edinburgh is perfectly acceptable, even though the genitive indicates the departure of the train, rather than the departure of Edinburgh! This is an example of the so-called **group genitive**, where the genitive phrase contains **postmodification**. Other examples are: [*the mayor of Chicago's*] *re-election campaign*, [*someone else's*] *fault*. However, although such examples are possible, the most common type of genitive consists of just one noun: particularly a proper noun, and more particularly the name of a person: [*Napoleon's*] *horse*, [*Marion's*] *husband*, and so on. Sometimes the noun following the genitive is omitted: *This scarf must be **your sister's***. The genitive forms of personal pronouns (for example, *my*, *your*, *his*) are known as **possessive** pronouns or determiners. (See **case; possessive pronoun**.)

**genitive pronouns**    see **possessive pronouns**

**gerund**    A traditional term used in reference to the *-ing* form of a verb when it has a noun-like function: *They're fond of **dancing***. In this book, the **-*ing* form** is a general term for words called either 'gerund' or 'present participle' in traditional approaches to grammar.

**gerund-participle, gerund-participial clause**    An alternative terminology for **-*ing* form, -*ing* clause**.

***get*-passive**    see **passive**

**given and new information**    A classification of the information conveyed by a sentence, clause or other grammatical unit. Given information is information already assumed to be known by the audience or reader, and new information is information not previously known and therefore to be particularly brought to the hearer's or reader's attention. In speech, new information is signalled by intonation and stress. For example, in the following exchange, the words in capitals represent important new information and are also the words which are likely to be strongly stressed:

(a)   Will the match take place TOMORROW?
(b)   Well, it MAY do, but I hope it will be POSTPONED.

There is a tendency to place new information after given information, that is to save up the important new information to the end of a sentence or clause. However, a speaker can vary the position of old and new information by varying the position of stress. Notice, for example, the difference of effect between (a) above and the same sentence (c) with a different major stress:

(c)   Will the match TAKE PLACE tomorrow?

(See **end focus**.)

**gradable adjectives**    see **adjective; gradable word**

**gradable word**    A word that can easily be used in the **comparative** or **superlative**, or is capable of being modified by an **adverb of degree** such as *very, much, greatly, considerably, rather* and *little*. For example, the adjectives *tall* and *beautiful* are gradable, because they have comparative and superlative forms (*taller ~ tallest, more beautiful ~ most beautiful*), also because they can be modified by *very*, and so on: *very tall, very beautiful*. In contrast, the adjectives *double* and *female* are non-gradable, since we cannot normally say \*doubler, \*more female, \*very double, \*rather female, and so on. Many adjectives are gradable, and so are some adverbs and determiners (for example, *often, easily, many, much*). Sometimes the same word may be gradable in one context but not in another. For example, *human* in a *human being* or *human history* is **non-gradable**. But we can say of a dog that its behaviour is very human, meaning that it behaves very much like a human being.

**grammatical concord**    see **notional concord**

**grammatical words**    see **function words**; compare **lexical words**.

**group genitive**    see **genitive**

---

H

**head**    The main word in a phrase. The head of a **noun phrase** is (normally) a **noun** or a **pronoun**. The head of an **adjective phrase** is an **adjective**. The head of an **adverb phrase** is an **adverb**.

The head of a phrase is an obligatory element, and other words, phrases or clauses are optionally added to it to qualify its meaning. These optional elements are called **modifiers**. For example, in *(friendly)* **places** *(to stay)*, *(extremely)* **tall** and *(more)* **often** *(than I expected)*, the parts in parentheses are modifiers, and those in bold are the heads of their phrases. (In this book we do not talk of heads and modifiers in verb phrases and prepositional phrases, but in some versions of grammar these phrases are also analysed in terms of heads and modifiers.) (See **modifier; phrase**.)

**historic present**    The use of the **present tense** in referring to **past time**, for example: *At that moment in **comes** a message from the Head Office, telling me the boss wants to see me in a hurry*. The historic present is sometimes used to create a vivid impression in popular oral narrative, and also occasionally in novels and short stories.

**hypothetical**    see **hypothetical; past tense; subjunctive**

**hypothetical past**    The use of the **past tense** to refer to an event or state of affairs which is not real. The event or state is seen as happening in some imaginary circumstances (past, present or future), rather than in the world of fact, for example in unreal **conditional clauses**: *If the principal knew about it, she would be furious*. The implication of this sentence is that the principal does not know about it. The past **modal auxiliaries** are often hypothetical, for example *I **couldn't** live with a man like that: it **would** be a nightmare*. To combine hypothetical meaning with past time, we use the past perfect: *Thanks for your help – I don't know what I **would have done** without you*. In this example, the speaker is clearly thinking of an imaginary situation in the past – a situation where the hearer had not offered help. (See **past tense**.)

## I

*if*-clause    see **conditional clause**

**imperative**    A form of the verb used to express a command or directive, that is something which the speaker requires the hearer to do. For this purpose, English always uses the **base form** of the verb (the form without any ending or inflection), for example: *take, look, send, let, prepare*. The imperatives of the primary verbs are *be, have* and *do*. When used for commands, the imperative can be impolite: *Sit down*; *Come here*. This can be softened a little by adding *please*: *Please sit down. Come here, please*. However, the imperative can also be used without impoliteness for invitations, good wishes and so on: *Take a look at this! Have a good time. Enjoy yourselves*. To make a negative imperative, we add *Don't* at the beginning: *Don't be silly. Don't make a mess*. In addition, we can add the emphatic auxiliary *Do* at the beginning to make the imperative more insistent in tone: *Do make yourself comfortable* is an insistent invitation.

The term imperative is used not only for the imperative verb itself but also for a clause or sentence having such a verb. Imperative sentences normally have no **subject**, but the implied subject is *you*, as we see when the reflexive pronoun *yourself* or *yourselves* is used as an object: *Behave yourself. Make yourselves at home.* In exceptional cases, we use *you* (stressed) as overt subject: *You be quiet.* Occasionally other subjects (such as names or indefinite pronouns) are also used: *Everyone sit down. Somebody make a pot of tea.* Another form of imperative has the initial word *Let's*: *Let's go for a swim.* This is a first-person imperative, which urges an action to be taken by both hearer(s) and speaker.

**imperfective**    see **perfective**

**impersonal**    Avoiding reference to human participants in a discourse. For example, the construction with *It* in *It is horrible that the accident happened on Claire's birthday* is impersonal: it makes no direct reference to the speaker, the hearer and their feelings. If the sentence began with *I'm horrified that* . . . or *You must be horrified* . . . then it would no longer be impersonal because of its reference to the speaker or the hearer. See **extraposition**.

**inclusive *we***    The use of *we* to include reference to the hearer(s) as well as the speaker. For example, *we* means 'you and I' in *You and I must have a talk. When shall **we** meet?* If *we* does not have this meaning, it is termed 'exclusive' (**exclusive *we***), as in: *We look forward to seeing you* (where *we* = 'the speaker and others'). (See **first person pronouns**.)

**indefinite article**    The word *a* (before consonants) or *an* (before vowels). *A/an* is only used with singular **count nouns** (compare **zero article**). It is a **determiner**, and normally occurs at the beginning of a **noun phrase**. As indefinite article, *a/an* contrasts with the **definite article** *the*: it is used to introduce a noun phrase referring to something or somebody who has not been mentioned or whose identity is not (yet) known to the hearer or reader. For instance: *I've just bought a car. Do you have a pencil? Her dad's an old friend of mine. A/an* is also used (for example, after *be*)

to describe or classify people or objects: *My mother's a teacher.*
*An arquebus is an old-fashioned firearm.* Historically, *a/an* is a
reduced form of the word *one*, and it is often used instead of *one*
in expressions like *a hundred*, *an hour and a half*, and the like.
(See **articles; generic**.)

**indefinite pronoun, indefinite determiner**    A **pronoun** or **determiner** with indefinite meaning; a quantifier. The indefinite
pronouns and determiners in English are:

pronouns:

| | | | |
|---|---|---|---|
| *anybody* | *everybody* | *nobody* | *somebody* |
| *anyone* | *everyone* | *no one* | *someone* |
| *anything* | *everything* | *nothing* | *something* |
| *none* | | | |

determiners:

| | | |
|---|---|---|
| *a/an* | *every* | *no* |

both pronouns and determiners:

| | | | | | |
|---|---|---|---|---|---|
| *any* | *either* | *fewest* | *least* | *much* | *some* |
| *all* | *enough* | *half* | *many* | *neither* | |
| *both* | *(a) few* | *(a) little* | *more* | *one* | |
| *each* | *fewer* | *less* | *most* | *several* | |

**independent and dependent clauses**    An independent **clause** is one
which is not part of (that is, is not subordinate to) another clause.
For example, in the coordinate sentence:

(a)  [He scored a goal], and [everybody cheered].

both the clauses linked by *and* are independent. But in the
sentence:

(b)  [[When he scored the goal], everybody cheered].

the clause beginning with *when* is dependent, being an **adverbial**
part of the main (independent) clause. In the sentence:

(c)  [¹ I thought [² that he was joking [³ when he said that ³]²]¹],
     but [⁴ I was wrong ⁴].

clauses 2 and 3 are dependent clauses, but clauses 1 and 4 are independent. Compare **main clause; subordinate clause**. 'Main' is sometimes used in an equivalent sense to 'independent', and 'subordinate' in an equivalent sense to 'dependent'. Here, however, we make a principled distinction between them.

**indicative mood**    see **mood**

**indirect object**    An **object** (**noun phrase**) which normally follows the main verb and precedes the direct object. For example:

> She gave *each of us* €100.
> I'm going to cook *you all* a light lunch.

The indirect object usually refers to someone indirectly affected by the action of the verb, for example a recipient or beneficiary. The same idea can often be expressed by a phrase beginning with *to* or *for*: *She gave €100 **to each of us**. I'm going to cook lunch **for you all**.* The indirect object can become the subject of a **passive**: *Each of us was given €100. We were given a beautiful present.* (See **direct object; object**.)

**indirect speech**    see **reported speech**

**infinitival clause**    see **infinitive, infinitive clause**

**infinitive**    The **base form** of the verb (that is the form without any suffix or inflection) used as a **non-finite verb**. For example, *be, have, do, see, regret* are infinitives when they follow a **modal auxiliary** or *do*: *may be, could have, can't do, might see, don't regret.* Also, the infinitive is used as the verb (or first verb) of a **non-finite clause**, where it is often preceded by *to*:

> I came [to *ask* you a favour].
> They wanted [to *be* met at the station].
> [To *have* escaped alive] was an amazing achievement.

The term infinitive is used (a) for the verb form itself (for example, *be*, *have*), (b) for the **verb phrase** (for example, *to be met*, *to have escaped*) and (c) for the clause (for example, *to be met at the station*, *to have escaped alive*) which has the infinitive verb phrase. (See **bare infinitive; non-finite verb; *to*-infinitive.**)

**infinitive clause**    see **infinitive; non-finite clause; *to*-infinitive**

**inflection** (or inflexion)    A change in the form of a word which signals a different grammatical function of the same word. The regular inflections in English are endings (suffixes) such as *-ed*, *-(e)s* or *-ing* added to the **base form** of a **regular verb**: *want*, *wanted*, *wants*, *wanting*. Other inflections take the form of a change of vowel, with or without the addition of a suffix: for example, in the irregular verb **write**, *wrote* and *written* are the **past tense** and *-ed* **participle** forms. We distinguish inflectional suffixes from derivational suffixes (see **derivational morphology**), which derive one word from another. For example, the *-s* of *boys* is inflectional, forming the plural of the same **noun**. But the *-ish* of *boyish* is derivational, forming another word (an **adjective**) from the noun *boy*. (See **irregular plurals; irregular verbs.**)

**inflectional morphology**    see **morphology**

**informal**    see **formal and informal**

**information (packaging)**    see **given and new information**

**-*ing* clause**    A type of **clause** in which the first (or only) verb word is an **-*ing* form**: *coming home*; *not doing the job properly*; *having been a teacher*; *visiting the park*. All -*ing* clauses are **non-finite clauses,** normally subordinate to other clauses. They have varied functions:

(a)  We met a lot of traffic [coming home].
(b)  He was accused of [not doing the job properly].
(c)  [Having been a teacher], you will know what kids are like.

(d)  The people [visiting the park] enjoy [walking among the flower beds].

In (a), *coming home* is an **adverbial clause** (of time). In (b), the *-ing* clause is a **nominal clause**. In (c) *Having been a teacher* is again an adverbial clause (of cause or reason). In (d), the first *-ing* clause is an **adjectival clause,** similar to the **relative clause** *who visit the park*, and the second is a nominal clause, acting as **object** of *enjoy*. Although a typical *-ing* clause usually has no **subject**, its implied subject is usually clear from the context. Sometimes, however, we place an overt subject in front of the *-ing* form:

(e)  I'm fed up with [*these trains being late*].
(f)  [*Weather permitting*], the competition will be held in the open.

In more formal English, the subject of a nominal *-ing* clause is sometimes a **genitive** or a **possessive pronoun**: *The flight delay was due to* [*its being the peak holiday season*]. An *-ing* clause is sometimes called a 'present participle construction' (especially when it is adjectival, as in (d)), or a 'gerund(ival) construction' (when it is nominal). (See *-ing* **form; non-finite clause.**)

*-ing* **form**    The form of the verb ending in *-ing*, for example: *being, doing, sending, increasing*. It is a **non-finite** form of the verb and is added to *be* to make the progressive construction: *is eating, were making, has been increasing* and so on. It can also be used as the only (or first) word of a **verb phrase** and as the first word of an *-ing* clause: [*Buying clothes*] *is what I enjoy most. She loves* [*being taken to the races*]. The *-ing* form is sometimes called a 'present participle' or (when it is in a nominal clause) a 'gerund'. The *-ing* form, as a form of a verb, should be distinguished from **nouns** and **adjectives** ending in *-ing* (for example, *a new* **building***, an* **interesting** *book*).

**instrument adverb/adverbial**    see **adjunct; adverbial**

**integrated relative clause**    Another term for a **restrictive relative clause**

**intensification**    A general term for the use of **degree adverbs** or **degree adverbials** to intensify the meaning or force of some part of a sentence. This can apply to the intensification of **adjectives** and **adverbs** (*immensely* hot, **very** *occasionally*) and also, for example, to the intensification of negative words and question words: *I'm not **in the least** hungry. What **on earth** were you thinking about?* Compare **emphasis.**

**intensifier**    An alternative term for a **degree adverb**, especially one which intensifies or strengthens the meaning of the word it modifies (for example, *very, extremely, really*).

**interjection**    A word which has a purely exclamatory function, such as *oh, ah, aha, ugh, ooh, alas, hey*. Interjections do not refer to anything, but simply express the speaker's emotion or wish. In grammatical terms, they occur in isolation as an **exclamation**, or are loosely added on to a sentence as in *Oh, it was wonderful!*

**interrogative**    Having a question function. The main types of interrogative sentences are *yes-no* questions, *wh*-questions, and **alternative questions**. (Subordinate interrogative clauses are discussed under *wh*-**clause** and **reported speech**. Interrogative words are discussed under *wh*-**word**.) (See **question**.)

**interrogative clause**    see **clause**

**intransitive**    see **transitive verb**

**intransitive verb**    A verb that does not require any object, complement or other element to complete its meaning. Thus, to complete a sentence, an intransitive verb can be added to the subject without any further addition: *Everyone laughed. The snow is falling.* But **adverbial** elements can be freely added after the intransitive verb: *Everyone laughed **at the joke**. The snow is falling heavily **in the north**.* (See **transitive verb**; **verb pattern**.)

**introductory *it*, introductory *there***    *It* and *there* used as introductory **subjects** in certain special kinds of sentence pattern. (See **cleft construction**; **existential *there***; **extraposition**.)

**inversion**    The reversal of the normal order of **subject** and **verb** word, so that the verb word precedes the subject. In English, we distinguish two kinds of inversion. Subject-operator inversion occurs where the **operator** (an auxiliary verb or the main verb *be*) is placed before the subject, for example in **questions** or in **statements** introduced by a negative word:

The weather is improving ~ *Is the weather* improving?
He did not say a word ~ Not a word *did he* say.

Subject-verb inversion occurs when the **main verb** (often the verb *be* or a simple verb of position or motion) is placed before the subject, in limited circumstances, especially when an adverbial of place introduces the sentence:

Your sister is there ~ There*'s your sister*.
The rain came down ~ Down *came the rain*.
The old city lies beneath the castle ramparts ~ Beneath the castle ramparts *lies the old city*.

(See ***wh*-question**; **yes-no question**.)

**irrealis**    A name for the **mood** of a verb that expresses 'unreal' or **hypothetical** meaning. In English grammatical usage, irrealis can be restricted to the use of *were* as a **subjunctive**.

**irregular plurals**    Noun **plurals** which do not follow the regular pattern of adding *-(e)s* to the singular. Common examples are:

| | | | |
|---|---|---|---|
| *man ~ men* | *foot ~ feet* | *sheep ~ sheep* | *wife ~ wives* |
| *woman ~ women* | *tooth ~ teeth* | *deer ~ deer* | *life ~ lives* |
| *child ~ children* | *goose ~ geese* | *mouse ~ mice* | *leaf ~ leaves* |
| *ox ~ oxen* | | | |

These are 'native' plurals, relics of an earlier stage of the English language. In addition, there are 'foreign' irregular plurals, such as those borrowed from Latin and Greek, for example, *stratum ~ strata*. (See **foreign plurals; plural**.)

**irregular verbs**    Verb words which do not form their **past tense** and *-ed* **participle** form in the regular way (see **verb**). There are over 200 irregular verbs in English, including many of the most common and important verbs in the language. In the following examples, (1) is the base form, (2) is the past tense form, and (3) is the *-ed* participle form:

| (1) | | (2) | | (3) | (1) | | (2) | | (3) |
|-----|---|-----|---|-----|-----|---|-----|---|-----|
| *be* | ~ | *was/were* | ~ | *been* | *bring* | ~ | *brought* | ~ | *brought* |
| *come* | ~ | *came* | ~ | *come* | *do* | ~ | *did* | ~ | *done* |
| *eat* | ~ | *ate* | ~ | *eaten* | *feel* | ~ | *felt* | ~ | *felt* |
| *give* | ~ | *gave* | ~ | *given* | *go* | ~ | *went* | ~ | *gone* |
| *have* | ~ | *had* | ~ | *had* | *know* | ~ | *knew* | ~ | *known* |
| *let* | ~ | *let* | ~ | *let* | *make* | ~ | *made* | ~ | *made* |
| *put* | ~ | *put* | ~ | *put* | *run* | ~ | *ran* | ~ | *run* |
| *say* | ~ | *said* | ~ | *said* | *see* | ~ | *saw* | ~ | *seen* |
| *sit* | ~ | *sat* | ~ | *sat* | *stand* | ~ | *stood* | ~ | *stood* |
| *tell* | ~ | *told* | ~ | *told* | *think* | ~ | *thought* | ~ | *thought* |

All English **auxiliary verbs** are irregular, and the verb *be*, the most common verb of all, is the most irregular of all. It has eight forms: *am, is, are, was, were, be, being, been*.

### L

**levels of style or usage**    see **formal and informal**

**lexical**    Relating to the lexicon (that is the dictionary or the vocabulary) of a language. A rough distinction is sometimes made between lexical words (or content words), whose meaning is explained in terms of their lexical content, and grammatical words (or **function words**), whose role is chiefly to be explained in terms of the grammar of a language. For example, **nouns** are lexical words and **articles** are grammatical words. The term 'lexical verb' is sometimes used for **main verbs**, as contrasted with **auxiliary verbs**.

**light verb**   A common and versatile lexical verb like *do*, *give*, *have*, *make* or *take*, which is semantically weak in many of its uses, and can be combined with nouns in constructions such as *do the cleaning*, *give (someone) a hug*, *have a drink*, *make a decision*, *take a break*. The whole construction often seems equivalent to the use of a single verb: *make a decision = decide*.

**linking adverbial** (also called **conjunct**)   An **adverbial** element whose main function is to link together two sentences, clauses and so on. Examples are: *however*, *nevertheless* (both expressing contrast), *moreover* (expressing addition), *otherwise* (expressing an alternative), *meanwhile* (expressing a link of time). These are all single-word adverbials, that is **adverbs**, but in other cases a linking adverbial may be a **phrase** or even a **clause**. For example, instead of *nevertheless*, we can use *all the same* or *in spite of that*, or instead of *moreover*, we can use *what is more*. Linking adverbials usually occur at the beginning of the sentence (or other unit) that they link to what precedes, but unlike **co-ordinating conjunctions** (such as *and*, *or* and *but*) they can occur also in the middle or at the end. All three of the following (a)–(c) might come after the sentence *Jason supports the animal rights campaign*:

(a)   However, his father disagrees with him.
(b)   His father, however, disagrees with him.
(c)   His father disagrees with him, however.

**linking words**   A general term for words which have a linking or connective role in grammar, such as **conjunctions**, **linking adverbials** and **copular verbs**.

M

**main clause**    A **clause** which has another clause (known as a **subordinate clause**) as part of it. For example, in

[The whole world hopes [that peace will prevail]].

the outer brackets enclose the main clause, and the inner brackets enclose another clause, a subordinate clause. The subordinate clause is part of the main clause. The following is a slightly more complex sentence in which there are three clauses, one inside the other:

[¹ I wonder [² if you could tell me [³ how she is ³]²].¹]

The clause marked 1 is definitely a main clause, and the clause marked 3 is definitely a subordinate clause. But clause 2 is both a main clause and a subordinate clause: it is a main clause from the point of view of clause 3, and a subordinate clause from the point of view of clause 1. In other words, we interpret main clause and subordinate clause as relative terms. Note the contrast between this and the distinction between **independent and dependent clauses**. (See also **subordinate clause**.)


**main verb**    A **verb** word which is not an **auxiliary verb** and which must occur in any normal clause or sentence (but see **verbless clause; ellipsis**). In the following **verb phrases**, the word in italics is the main verb:

| | | |
|---|---|---|
| *came* | *takes* | *is* |
| has *come* | are *taking* | *being* |
| has been *coming* | having been *taken* | may have *been* |

Note that the auxiliary verbs – those not in italics – always come before the main verb. Note also that the primary verbs *be*, *have* and *do* can be either an auxiliary or a main verb. When *be*, *have* or *do* is a main verb, it is the last (or only) verb in the verb phrase. Hence, in *Jack is asleep* or *Jack may have been asleep*, *be* is the main verb; but in *Jack is lying* or *Jack may have been lying*, *lie* is the main verb and *be* an auxiliary. The main verb is a pivotal word, to a great extent determining the structural and meaning relations within the clause. The term 'lexical verb' is sometimes used instead of main verb, but strictly speaking, 'lexical verb' excludes the primary verbs *be*, *have* and *do* even when they act as main verbs. (See **auxiliary verb**.)

**mandative subjunctive**    see **subjunctive**

**manner adverb/adverbial**    An **adverb** or **adverbial** whose meaning is 'in such-and-such a manner'. The most common manner adverbials are adverbs derived from adjectives, typically ending in *-ly*, for example *carefully*, *slowly*, *hungrily*, *unconsciously*. (However, many of the most common adverbs in *-ly*, like *really*, are not manner adverbs.) The **comparative** and **superlative** of manner adverbs are formed with *more* and *most*, for example *more slowly*, *most carefully*. A few manner adverbs are irregular: *well* (= 'good + ly'), *better*, *best*, *worse* (= 'more badly') and *worst*, as in *Paula plays the guitar **well**. Of the three children, Paula plays the guitar **best/worst**.* Manner adverbials answer the question 'How? In what manner?'

**marked and unmarked**    Where there is a contrast between two or more members of a category such as **number**, **case** or **tense**, one of them is called 'marked' if it contains some extra affix, as opposed to the 'unmarked' member which does not. For example, the **regular plural** (such as *tables*) of a noun is the marked form in comparison with the singular (*table*) because it has an extra affix, the *-s* (or *-es*) plural inflection. In a similar way, the ordinary form of an adjective such as *old* is unmarked in contrast to the **comparative** and **superlative** forms, *older* and *oldest*. By extension, the marked form can also be marked syntactically, by having more words. For example, the passive *was eaten* is marked in relation to the unmarked active *ate*. Generally the unmarked form is the more frequent option and also the one that has the most neutral meaning.

**masculine**    Having male, rather than female, reference (contrast **feminine**). Masculine, feminine and neuter forms traditionally make up the grammatical category of gender. However, gender has only a limited role in English grammar, being restricted to the third-person pronouns. The masculine pronouns in English are *he*, *him*, *his* and *himself*. (See **feminine**; **gender**; **personal pronoun**.)

**mass noun**    A noun which refers to substances (solids, liquids and gases) in the mass, for example *rice*, *milk*, *tar*, *smoke*. Mass nouns are non-count nouns. (See **count noun**; **non-count noun**.)

**matrix clause**    (1) Another term for a **main clause**.
(2) A term for a main clause *minus* the **subordinate clause**. Thus in:

[*You can drink your orange* [if you like]].

the main clause is enclosed by the outer brackets and the subordinate clause by the inner brackets. The matrix clause (2) is the part of the main clause which is in italics. Although a matrix clause, so defined, is not strictly speaking a **clause** at all, it is sometimes useful to distinguish it from the material in the subordinate clause.

**means adverb/adverbial**    see **adverbial**

**mid-position, middle position**    The position in which an adverbial is placed when it occurs in the middle of a clause. For example, the adverbs are in mid-position in: *The game will **soon** begin. Our friends **often** send us presents. The children were **fortunately** in bed.* The most usual mid-position is (a) just after the **operator**, if any, (b) otherwise just after the **subject**.

**minor sentence (type)**    see **verbless sentence**

**modal (auxiliary) (verb)**    A member of a small class of verbs that have meanings relating to modality, that is to such concepts as possibility or permission (*can*, *may*), obligation, necessity or likelihood (*must*, *should*), prediction, intention or hypothesis (*will*, *would*). The modal auxiliaries group in pairs, except for *must*:

| | | | | |
|---|---|---|---|---|
| *will ('ll)* | *can* | *may* | *shall* | *must* |
| *would ('d)* | *could* | *might* | *should* | |

The lower modals in the list above are historically the past tense forms of the upper modals, but nowadays they have developed independent uses (especially *would* and *should*). The modals always function as **operators**, and occur in first position in their **verb phrase**. They form a construction with the **bare infinitive** of another verb, for example *may be*, *may have*, *may find*. They have no other forms, such as *-s* forms, *-ing* forms or *-ed* forms. They are placed before the subject to form questions and before *not* in negation:

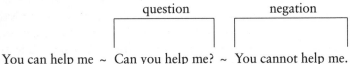

| question | | negation |
|---|---|---|

You can help me  ~  Can you help me?  ~  You cannot help me.
We will succeed  ~  Will we succeed?  ~  We will not succeed.

Except for *may*, modals can also express negation by negative **contractions**: *won't*, *can't*, *shan't*, *mustn't*, *wouldn't*, *couldn't*, *mightn't*, *shouldn't*: *You can't help me. We won't succeed.* Modals are very widely used in conversation for expressing various kinds of speech acts such as requests (*Could I use your phone? Would you mind signing this form?*), offers (*Can we offer you a lift?*) and promises (*I'll call you back this afternoon.*) Some less important verbs (*ought to*, *used to*, *need*, *dare*) are sometimes included with the modals because of their similar meanings and/or grammatical behaviour. (See **auxiliary verb**; **operator**.)

**modality**    see **modal (auxiliary verb)**.

**modifier**   A word, phrase, or clause which is added to another word to specify more precisely what it refers to. For example, in the following phrases, the expressions in italics are modifiers:

(a)   a *new* house *in the country*                    (**noun phrase**)
(b)   something *which I bought recently*        (**noun phrase**)
(c)   *amazingly* beautiful                                (**adjective phrase**)
(d)   often *enough*                                          (**adverb phrase**)

The words *house, something, beautiful* and *often* in these examples are termed the **heads** of their respective phrases. Modifiers preceding the head are called **premodifiers** (for example, *new* in (a)). Modifiers following the head are called **postmodifiers** (for example, *in the country* in (a)). In noun phrases, adjective phrases and adverb phrases, modifiers are optional elements which add specification to the meaning of the head. Thus a phrase may contain no modifiers, one modifier, or several modifiers.

**mood**   A verb category which is not so useful in the grammar of English as it is for some other languages and has to do with the degree of reality attributed to the happening described by the verb. The indicative mood (that of normal finite forms of the verb) contrasts with the 'unreality' of the **subjunctive** mood. The **imperative, infinitive** and **interrogative** are also sometimes considered to be moods of the verb.

**morphology**   The part of grammar (and lexicology) which analyses the structure of words. Morphology is a relatively un-important part of English grammar because English words have relatively few **inflections** (that is changes in the form of a word determined by its grammatical role). The suffixes of **nouns** (*-s*), **verbs** (*-ed, -ing, -s*) and **adjectives** (*-er, -est*), leaving aside some marginal and irregular forms, make up the total of English in-flectional morphology. Inflectional morphology is distinguished from derivational morphology, which deals with the formation of words from other existing words, and belongs to lexicology rather than grammar. However, derivational morphology is relevant to grammar because derivational suffixes such as *-ness* (for nouns), *-ful* (for adjectives) and *-ly* (for adverbs) help us to recognize the members of grammatical word classes. Morphology contrasts with **syntax**.

N

**name, naming expression**    A word or phrase which refers to a specific person, place, group, and so on. The simplest naming expressions are proper nouns such as *Jane, Robinson, Moscow, Africa*. Other naming expressions may contain sequences of such names (*Nelson Mandela*), names preceded by titles (*Mr Tom McKenzie*), proper nouns followed by common nouns (*the Atlas Mountains*) and so on. Naming expressions are spelt with initial capitals on important (especially **lexical** or **open class**) words, and are sometimes reduced to initials or acronyms, for example, the *UN, OPEC, the PRC*.

**nationality word**    A noun or adjective identifying one particular country or its inhabitants. For example, *Sweden* (**proper noun**), *Swedish* (adjective), *Swede* (**common noun** referring to an individual of Swedish nationality). Nationality words are spelt with an initial capital letter, even when they are adjectives or common nouns.

**negation, negative**    Negation is the operation of changing a sentence or other unit into its negative form, especially by using *not*. The normal form of negation in English is to add *not* (or its contracted form *-n't*) after the **operator** (that is, after the first **auxiliary verb** or the **finite verb** *be*):

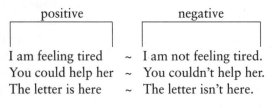

| positive | | negative |
|---|---|---|
| I am feeling tired | ~ | I am not feeling tired. |
| You could help her | ~ | You couldn't help her. |
| The letter is here | ~ | The letter isn't here. |

When the positive sentence has no operator, *do* is used as a **dummy** operator to form the negative:

Sue likes jogging    ~  Sue *doesn't* like jogging.

The contracted negative forms are used in informal style, especially in speech. They are: *isn't, aren't, wasn't, weren't, hasn't, haven't, hadn't, doesn't, don't, didn't, won't, shan't, can't, mustn't, wouldn't, shouldn't, couldn't, mightn't.* For some operators there is no negative contraction (for example, *may not, am not*) and so the full form has to be used. In making a sentence or clause negative, we sometimes have to make other changes. For example, it is common to replace *some* by *any* when it follows *not*. The negative of *We saw some rare birds* is *We didn't see any rare birds.* (See **negative word; non-assertive; transferred negation.**)

**negative**    see **negation; positive; negative concord**

**negative concord**    A term sometimes used instead of 'double negative' or 'multiple negative' for the construction in which two or more negative words occur in the same clause, but the meaning of the clause is that of a single negative:

He did*n't* say *nothing.*
She *ain't never* given me *no* problems.

In English, unlike some other languages, negative concord is a feature of vernacular grammar not acceptable in the standard language. The standard way to reformulate the sentences above is:

He did*n't* say *anything.*
She has*n't ever* given me *any* problems.

**negative word**    A word which has the function of negating the meaning of a clause or sentence. Apart from the most important negative word *not* – sometimes called a negative **particle** – other negative words include *no* (determiner or response form); *none, nobody, no one, nothing* (pronouns); *never, nowhere* (adverbs). The functions of these are similar to that of *not*: to say *Nobody was asleep* is to say the same as *Everyone was not asleep*, that is *Everyone was awake*. When a negative word comes later than the subject of the sentence, it can usually be replaced by *not* with a **non-assertive** word such as *any, anyone, ever*: *I have never learned to ski = I haven't ever learned to ski*.

**neuter** (or non-personal)    Having neither **masculine** nor **feminine gender**. *It*, in contrast to *he* and *she*, is a neuter pronoun.

**new information**    see **given and new information**

**nominal**    (1) The adjective corresponding to 'noun': it means 'noun-like'.
    (2) As a noun, 'nominal' is used for a constituent of a noun phrase intermediate in extent between a **noun phrase** and a **noun**. For example, in the noun phrase *a nice cup of tea*, it makes sense to say that *nice* is a modifier of *cup of tea*, rather than just the head noun *cup*. Hence we can say that *cup of tea* is a nominal, which is larger than a single noun but smaller than the whole noun phrase.

**nominal clause** (also called **noun clause** or – with a slightly different meaning – **complement clause**)    A subordinate clause which has a function in the sentence similar to that of a **noun phrase**. Like noun phrases, nominal clauses can act as **subject**, **object** or **complement** of the main clause:

> [*What you do*] does not concern me.    (subject)
> I didn't ask [*where you live*].    (object)
> The hope is [*that we will succeed*].    (complement)

Some nominal clauses can also occur after a **preposition**: *It all depends on* [*how you feel*]. **Finite** nominal clauses include *that*-clauses, *wh*-interrogative clauses and **nominal relative clauses**.

There are also plenty of **non-finite** nominal clauses, for example the **-*ing* clauses** or **infinitive clauses**:

[*Sending him money now*] would be like [*putting the cart before the horse*].
[*To send him money now*] would be [*to put the cart before the horse*].

**nominal group**    An alternative term for a **noun phrase**.

**nominal relative clause**    A relative clause which has no **antecedent** and which is therefore equivalent, in its function in the sentence, to a whole noun phrase. For example, it fills the **subject** slot in [*What you need most*] *is a good stiff drink*. Here *What you need most* means the same as 'The thing which you need most'. Nominal relative clauses begin with a ***wh*-word**, often a ***wh-ever* word** like *whoever*: *I want to speak to* [*whoever answered the phone just now*] (that is, 'the person who answered the phone just now').

**nominalization**    A **noun phrase** which has the underlying semantic structure of a **clause**. An example of nominalization is *the destruction of the city*, where the noun *destruction* corresponds to the **main verb** of a clause and *the city* to its **object**: '(Someone or something) destroyed the city'. The **subject** of the underlying clause can be expressed by a genitive and **adverbs** can be represented in the noun phrase by **adjectives**: *Hannibal's sudden arrival in the city* = 'Hannibal suddenly arrived in the city'.

**nominative**    A traditional term for the **subjective case**. Compare **objective case**.

**non-affirmative, non-assertive**    These two terms have the same meaning: lacking positive, affirmative meaning. Questions and negative statements tend to be non-assertive, in contrast to positive statements. This means that quantifiers such as *any, anyone*, *anything* (so-called *any*-words) tend to be used in them, in contrast to *some*, *someone*, *something*, and so on. Compare:

I've watched *some* good games recently.         (assertive)
Have you watched *any* good games recently?   (non-assertive)
I haven't watched *any* good games recently.   (non-assertive)

The rule which replaces *some* by *any* and so forth is not absolute. There are, in fact, 'assertive questions' which contain words like *some*: *Have you watched some good games recently?* (These are 'loaded questions' expecting a positive reply.) Words like *any* can be termed non-assertive items. They include not only *any* and words beginning with *any*-, but also *ever*, *yet* and *at all*.

**non-clausal unit**   see **verbless sentence**

**non-count noun** (also called uncountable noun)   A **noun** which has no plural use and which cannot be used with 'counting' words such as *one*, *two*, *three*, *a few* and *many*. Examples are **mass nouns** like *bread*, *milk*, *leather*, *steam*, *gold* which refer to substances and materials. But also many **abstract nouns** are non-count: for example, *advice*, *health*, *music*, *sanity*. Non-count nouns contrast with **count nouns**, such as *street*, *table*, *child*, *meeting*. However, this contrast is oversimplified, since many nouns can be either count or non-count according to meaning (compare *some paper* ~ *some papers*, *a lot of change* ~ *a lot of changes*). Also, nouns that are primarily non-count can be used as count nouns in special contexts. For example, *a little sugar* (= mass substance) is normal, but *a few sugars* could be used to mean either a few lumps of sugar or a few types of sugar.

**non-defining relative clause**   see **restrictive and non-restrictive relative clauses**

**non-finite**   see **auxiliary verb; bare infinitive; -*ing* form; non-finite clause; participle; predication; verb phrase**

**non-finite clause**    A clause which has a non-finite verb phrase (see **non-finite verb** below). Non-finite clauses are subdivided into (a) **infinitive clauses**, (b) *-ing* **clauses** and (c) *-ed* **clauses**. For example:

(a)    This is the best way [*to serve dressed crab*].
(b)    They have an odd way of [*serving dressed crab*].
(c)    The dressed crab [*served in this restaurant*] is excellent.

Non-finite clauses are normally **subordinate clauses**. They are treated as clauses because they have elements such as **subject, verb, object** and **adverbial**. However, as in the examples above, although its meaning is implied, the subject of a non-finite clause is usually omitted. (See **finite clause; finite verb**.)

**non-finite nominal clause**    see **nominal clause**

**non-finite verb**    A verb form which is not **finite**, that is does not involve variation for **past tense** and **present tense**. The three non-finite verb forms are (a) the **infinitive**, with or without *to*, (b) the *-ing* **form** (often called **present participle** or **gerund**) and (c) the *-ed* **form** (**past participle**):

| (a) | | (b) | | (c) | |
|---|---|---|---|---|---|
| | *(to) be* | | *being* | | *been* |
| | *(to) eat* | | *eating* | | *eaten* |
| | *(to) live* | | *living* | | *, lived* |

All verbs, except for **modal auxiliaries**, have non-finite forms. Non-finite forms always follow the finite verb form (if any) in the verb phrase: *will be, is eating, has lived, has been living, will be eating* and so on. Such verb phrases are called finite because they begin with the finite verb form. But, in addition, non-finite verb forms occur in non-finite verb phrases which do not contain a finite verb. Types of non-finite verb phrases are (a) infinitive phrases (beginning with an infinitive form), (b) *-ing* phrases (beginning with an *-ing* form) and (c) *-ed* phrases (beginning with an *-ed* form). Examples of non-finite verb phrases are:

| (a) | *to eat* | (b) | *eating* | (c) | *eaten* |
|-----|----------|-----|----------|-----|---------|
|     | *to be eating* |  | *having eaten* |  | *seen* |
|     | *to have sent* |  | *having been eaten* |  | *answered* |

Modal auxiliaries like *can* are considered to be finite, because they come first in the verb phrase and have (at least to some extent) the present/past contrast of *can ~ could*, and so on. (See **finite verb**.)

**non-finite verb phrases**    see **non-finite verb; perfect** (*Table* 3)

**non-personal**    An alternative term for **neuter**.

**non-restrictive**    A modifier that is non-restrictive adds meaning to a noun phrase in a way which does not restrict or limit its reference. (See **restrictive and non-restrictive relative clauses**.)

**notional concord**    Concord (or agreement) where the choice of **verb** form is determined more by the meaning of the **subject** than by the strict grammatical concord between singular and singular, plural and plural. For example, with **collective nouns**, both of the following are acceptable:

The audience *was* impressed by his performance.
The audience *were* impressed by his performance.

The first sentence illustrates grammatical concord (singular verb with singular subject); the second (plural verb with singular subject) breaks grammatical concord, but observes notional concord. The notion of 'plurality' is present in the singular subject, since an audience can be easily thought of as consisting of a set of separate people. (See **concord**.)

**noun**    A very large class of words which refer to entities (persons, things, substances, places and abstractions of various kinds). A noun can be the head of a **noun phrase** and therefore the chief word in indicating the **subject** or **object** of a verb. Most **common**

**nouns** have both a singular and a plural form, the regular **plural** being shown by the addition of *-(e)s* to the singular form: *boy ~ boys, cat ~ cats, church ~ churches, kindness ~ kindnesses* and so on. (There are also some **irregular plurals** such as *woman ~ women, life ~ lives, sheep ~ sheep, formula ~ formulae*.) Nouns are subdivided into the following major categories: **common nouns** contrast with **proper nouns**; **count nouns** contrast with **non-count nouns** (including **mass nouns**); **concrete nouns** contrast with **abstract nouns**; **collective nouns** contrast with non-collective nouns. Many words can be recognized as nouns by their suffixes, for example *-ion* (in *action*), *-er* (in *reader*), *-or* (in *actor*), *-ness* (in *business*), *-ity* (in *authority*), *-ment* (in *department*) and *-ship* (in *friendship*). (See **noun phrase**.)

**noun clause**    see **nominal clause**

**noun phrase**    A **phrase** which (typically) has a **noun** or a **pronoun** as its **head** and which can have various important functions in a clause or sentence, notably those of **subject, object, complement** or **prepositional complement**. (Certain kinds of noun phrases – especially time phrases like *last week* – can also be **adverbials**.) The structure of noun phrases can be stated simply as follows: (**determiner**[s]) + (**modifier**[s]) + **head** + (**modifier**[s]) where brackets represent optional elements. Very often the phrase consists of a head alone – either a **noun** or a **pronoun** (for example, *her, music, animals*): these could all be objects of a sentence beginning *I love* . . . The next most frequent type of noun phrase consists of a determiner (especially one of the **articles** *the* and *a/an*) with a following noun, as in *the music, an animal, those animals*. Before a singular **count noun**, there must be a determiner (for example, *animal* without a determiner cannot be a noun phrase: *\*I saw animal*). To form more complex noun phrases, **modifiers** of various kinds may be added either before or after the noun head. One-word modifiers, especially adjectives and nouns, typically occur before the head: *a hungry child, Russian folk music, these lively young animals*. On the other hand, multi-word modifiers, especially **prepositional phrases** and **relative clauses**, generally occur after the head: *the music [of Beethoven]*; *the music [that I love best]*; *the music [of Beethoven] [that I love best]*. Naturally, the modifiers which precede and which follow the head can be combined in one noun phrase so that noun phrases of great length can be built up: *the recent unrest in Ruritania, which has led to a cautious measure of liberalization in a regime that up to recently has been a byword for totally inflexible authoritarianism* is a single noun phrase. As this example shows, noun phrases can become complex not only through combinations of different kinds of modifiers, but through the embedding of one phrase or clause in another. Noun phrases are so varied in their form that they allow some structures which are exceptions to the general rules given above. For example, multi-word modifiers can precede the head in the form of a genitive phrase: *[my mother's] friends*. Also, there are cases where the head of a noun phrase is an adjective: *the rich*; *the unemployed*; *the good, the bad and the indifferent*; and so on.

**noun-pronoun concord**    see **concord**

**nucleus**    The part of a clause or sentence that consists of **subject** and **predicate**. In the simplest and most straightforward cases, the nucleus corresponds to the whole clause. But in more complex clause structures, there are additional elements more loosely related to the rest of the clause. See **prenucleus.**

**null**    see **gap; zero**

**number**    (1) The grammatical choice between **singular** (one) and **plural** (more than one). In English, **nouns, pronouns, determiners** and **present tense verbs** can vary for number, for example: *student ~ students, I ~ we, that ~ those, takes ~ take.*
    (2) Another term for a numeral. (See **numerals**.)

**numerals** (also called numbers)    Words referring to number. The two main classes of numerals are **cardinal numerals** (*one, two, three, four . . .*) and **ordinal numerals** (*first, second, third, fourth . . .*). They may be written not only in letters, but in digits: *1, 2, 3, 4, . . . 15, . . . 66, . . . 1,000, . . .* or *1st, 2nd, 3rd, 4th, . . . 15th, . . . 66th, . . .* and so on. Numerals have a small grammar of their own within the larger grammar of the English language. For example, speakers of English know how to read aloud the numeral *11,362* (*eleven thousand three hundred and sixty-two*) even though they have probably not met with that particular number before. As for their grammatical function in sentence grammar, numerals behave rather like **determiners** and **pronouns**. Like determiners, they can precede the **modifiers** and **head** of a **noun phrase**: *three blind mice, our twenty-ninth wedding anniversary*. (However, they follow most determiners when co-occurring with them in the same noun phrase: *the Ten Commandments, her fourth child*.) Like pronouns, they can also occupy the position of head of a noun phrase:

Those delicious cakes! I have already eaten *three*.
Really? This is only my *second*.

In addition, ordinal numbers can be used like **adverbs**, for example: ***First, let me introduce my family. In the final race, Jason came* sixth**.

---

### O

**object**    A part of a clause or sentence which normally follows the **main verb** and corresponds to the **subject** of a **passive** clause or sentence. For example:

| | |
|---|---|
| Armadillos eat *termites*. | (*termites* is the object) |
| *Termites* are eaten by armadillos. | (*termites* is the subject of the passive) |

She actually bought *a can opener*.
Charles is visiting *the Joneses* tomorrow.

An object is usually a noun phrase (as in the examples above). If it is a personal pronoun, the **objective case** is needed: *me, him, her, us, them* – not *I, he, she, we, they*. An object can also be a **nominal clause**: *Everyone knows* [*that mercury is a metal*]. *People rarely believe* [*what she says*]. A useful way to identify an object is to consider it as an answer to a question with *What* or *Who(m)* + auxiliary + subject: *What do armadillos eat? Who(m) is Charles visiting tomorrow?* In terms of meaning, the object is often identified with the person, thing and so on that is affected by the action described by the verb. Whereas the subject typically represents the 'doer', the object typically represents the 'doee'. A clause may have an **indirect object** in addition to a **direct object**: in *Charles is cooking the family a meal*, *the family* is the indirect object (representing those who are indirectly affected by the action, in this case the beneficiaries) and *a meal* is the direct object. (See **complement**; **indirect object**; **passive**.)

**object complement**    A **complement**[1] which follows the **object**, and which describes some (putative) characteristic of what the object refers to. For example, in *Margaret has been keeping the house tidy*, *tidy* is the object complement and *the house* is the object. The relation between the object and object complement can be represented by the verb *be*: an implied meaning of the above sentence is that 'the house *is* tidy'. The object complement can be an **adjective** (or **adjective phrase**), as above, or it can be a **noun phrase**, as in: *The empress declared Catherine her heir*. The set of verbs which permit an object complement is not large. In addition to *keep* and *declare* (illustrated above), it includes *leave, call, like, want, consider, find, think, get, make, send, turn, elect* and *vote*. Compare **subject complement** (see **complement**).

**objective (case)**    The special form a pronoun takes when it has the role of **object** in a clause, for example *We admire her*. The objective forms of the personal pronouns are *me, him, her, us, them*, in contrast to the **subjective** forms *I, he, she, we, they*. (The *wh-*pronoun *who* also has an objective form *whom*, but *whom* is often avoided, even in object position, in favour of *who*.) The term 'objective' should not be taken to mean that these forms are found only in the object position: objective pronouns are also used following a **preposition** and frequently in other positions (especially as **subject complement**) and after *than*, in which the subjective form is traditionally considered correct: *Hello! It's only me. You've won more games than us.* (See **case**.) Alternative terms for 'objective' are 'accusative' and 'oblique'.

**oblique (case)**    see **objective (case)**

**omission**    see **ellipsis; gap; zero**

**open and closed word classes**    A major classification of **word classes** (also called 'parts of speech'). Open classes are those which have a very large membership, namely **nouns**, lexical **verbs**, **adjectives**, **adverbs** and (marginally) **numerals**. Closed classes, on the other hand, are those which have a rather small membership, namely **conjunctions**, **determiners**, **interjections**, **operator verbs**, **prepositions**, **pronouns**. The open classes are so called because it is easy to add new words to them by established processes of word formation, for example: *politisoap* (a new noun), *non-manic* (a new adjective), *Shakespearized* (a new verb) (examples are from British newspapers in 2003, from the website of the RDUES, University of Central England). In contrast, it is quite difficult to introduce (say) a new determiner or conjunction into the language. The distinction between open and closed classes is not absolute, and there is a scale of 'openness' in both categories: for example, in the closed category, prepositions are relatively open. (See **lexical**.)

**open interrogative clause**    Another name for *wh*-**interrogative clause** or *wh*-**question**.

**operator**    A verb word which has a key role in forming negative, interrogative and other types of 'derived' clauses or sentences in English. The class of operator verbs includes the **modal auxili-**

aries *will*, *can*, *may*, *shall*, *must*, *would*, *could*, *might*, *should*; the finite forms of the auxiliaries ***have*** and ***do***; and the finite forms of the verb ***be*** (both as an auxiliary and as a main verb). In addition, it includes the negative contractions of these verbs: *won't*, *can't*, *shan't*, *mustn't*, *wouldn't*, *mightn't*, *shouldn't*, *hasn't*, *haven't*, *hadn't*, *doesn't*, *don't*, *didn't*, *isn't*, *aren't*, *wasn't*, *weren't*. If we think of a 'basic' sentence pattern in the form of a positive statement, such as *The dog **has** eaten its dinner*, then it is easy to form (a) negative, (b) interrogative and (c) elliptical sentences by means of the operator as follows. (a) Place *not* after the operator or replace the operator by its negative contraction: *The dog **has** not* (or ***hasn't***) *eaten its dinner*. (b) Place the operator in front of the subject: ***Has/Hasn't** the dog eaten its dinner?* (c) Delete whatever follows the operator: (*The cat **hasn't** eaten its dinner, but*) *the dog **has***. An operator can be defined as either a finite auxiliary, or a finite form of the verb ***be***. It will be noted that some positive statements do not have an operator (namely, those with a finite main verb other than be). For the operator rules (a)–(c) to work, these positive statements must be replaced by equivalent statements in which the **dummy** operator do is introduced:

> It rained heavily last month. ~
> (It *did* rain heavily last month.)\*
> It *didn't* rain heavily last month.
> *Did/Didn't* it rain heavily last month?
> (They said it would rain heavily last month, and) it *did*.

The second sentence above, in parentheses and marked \*, does not occur except when the operator is pronounced with stress, often combined with pitch accent. (See **auxiliary; ellipsis; emphasis; finite verb.**)

**ordinal number/numeral**   see **cardinal number/numeral; numerals**

P

**paradigm**  A set of choices made from the same grammatical category. For example, the different forms of a regular verb – *look, looks, looked, looking* – form a paradigm; also the different forms of a personal pronoun – *I, me, my, mine*.

**parenthetical**  A parenthetical constituent of a sentence is one which is, so to speak, 'in parentheses' or 'in brackets'. This does not mean that the constituent can always be recognized by enclosure in ( ) or [ ]: other punctuation, such as commas and dashes in writing, or their prosodic equivalent in speech, can be used. A useful test for a parenthetical constituent is whether the constituent can be subtracted from the whole sentence without affecting the structure and meaning of the remainder. In some cases, the parenthetical structure itself can be a sentence:

. . . And at last – *I'll never forget the moment* – someone blew three shrill blasts on a trumpet. The ordeal was over.

**participial, participle**  Participle is a traditional term for the nonfinite *-ing* **form** and *-ed* **form** of the verb, especially when they are used in a quasi-adjectival way. Thus, in *They heard the children laughing* and *They heard the window being smashed/broken*, *laughing* and *being* are present participles and *smashed* and *broke*n are past (or passive) participles. They can also be called *-ing* participle and *-ed* participle. 'Participial' is the adjectival form of 'participle'. Compare **gerund**.

**particle**  A useful though rather vague term for a 'little word' (Latin 'little part') which does not belong to one of the regular word classes. For example, *not* can be called a 'negative particle'. In multi-word verbs like *make up*, *look after*, 'particle' is often used for one of the words which follow the main verb, for example *up*, *after*. (See **phrasal verb; prepositional verb**.)

**parts of speech**  A traditional term for **word classes** (such as **noun, verb, adjective, preposition**).

**passive, passive voice**   A type of verb construction in which a form of *be* is followed by the *-ed* **form** (past participle) of the main verb, for example *is loved, was beaten, will be sent*. Hence, a passive **clause** or sentence is one in which the **verb phrase** is passive. The effect of using the passive is to convert the noun phrase which would be the object of a corresponding non-passive (that is, active) clause into the subject. For example:

Police *have found* the missing children.            (active)
The missing children *have been found* by police.   (passive)

Thus the passive reverses the normal relation between the 'doer' and the 'done to'. The subject of the active clause (in this case, *the police*) corresponds to the **agent** (the noun phrase following *by*) in the passive. However, the agent is usually omitted: *The missing children have been found*. The passive is useful for various purposes. For example, if we want to place emphasis on the 'doer' as the most important piece of new information, the passive enables us to place the 'doer' after the verb, so giving it **end focus**. On the other hand, if we want to omit information about the 'doer', we can simply omit the agent. Strictly, however, the agent does not have to be the 'doer' or performer of an action. Some verbs, such as *see* and *know*, are not action verbs, but can still be used in the passive: *I'm known as Wild Willimina from Waco*. In informal English, there is also a *get*-passive in which the first verb is **get** instead of **be**: *I got fired yesterday for not attending to business*.

**past participial construction**   see *-ed* **clause**; **participle**

**past participle**   A traditional term for the non-finite *-ed* **form** of verbs. (See also **participle**; *-ed* **clause**.)

**past perfect** (also called pluperfect)   A form of **verb phrase**, consisting of *had* + *-ed* **form**, in which the **perfect** construction is combined with the **past tense**, for example *had lived, had left*, *had written*. The meaning of the past perfect is: happening before a time in the past, that is 'past in the past':

> The front door *had banged* shut and Saskia was waiting impatiently on the doorstep.

The past perfect can be combined with the **progressive** (for example, *Someone **had been eating** the cake*) or the passive (for example, *The cake **had been eaten***).

**past progressive**   A form of the **verb phrase** in which the **past tense** is combined with the **progressive** construction: it consists of a past tense of ***be*** + ***-ing* form**, for example *was leaving, were helping*. Its typical meaning is that something was 'going on', that is in progress, at a definite time in the past:

> Martha *was staying* at a hotel in Bath when she heard of her father's death.

The past progressive can be combined with the passive, for example *was being sold, were being taught*.

**past simple** (or simple past)   A form of the **verb phrase** in which there is just one verb – the **past tense** form of the main verb: *That evening, the police **came**. Moreland **asked** what it **meant**.* The term past simple also generally applies to corresponding interrogative and negative constructions, which, except with ***be***, require the corresponding form of the dummy operator, *did/didn't*. Compare, for example, *I **saw** it. ~ **Did(n't)** you see it? ~ I **didn't** see it.*

**past tense**   A form of the verb (for example, *saw, looked, found*) which contrasts with the present tense (for example, *see[s], look[s], find[s]*). The past tense indicates (a) that the happening took place at a definite time before the present, or else (b) that the happening is seen as unreal or hypothetical. For example:

(a)   Columbus went to America in 1492. (past time)

(b)  If Columbus went to America today, he would be utterly astonished. (unreal, hypothetical)

The regular past tense is formed by adding -ed (or -d) to the base form of the verb: *talk ~ talked*, *change ~ changed*. But there are over 200 irregular verbs (including all **auxiliary verbs**) which form the past tense differently, for example *see ~ saw*, *take ~ took*, *meet ~ met*. *Be* is the only verb which has more than one past tense form (ignoring contractions like *'d, didn't*): it has *was* (singular) and *were* (plural). A **verb phra**se can be made past by using the past tense of its first (**finite**) verb: *ate*, *was eating*, *had eaten*, *was being eaten* and so on. Some **modal auxiliaries** do not have a past tense form, for example *must*. Historically, other modals do have past tense forms (*may ~ might*, *will ~ would*), but the past tense forms behave almost like independent verbs.

**perfect** (**aspect**)    A verb construction consisting of ***have* + *-ed* form**, for example *has happened*, *has lived*, *have eaten*. The perfect contrasts with non-perfect (for example, present simple or past simple) forms, and its meaning places the happening in a preceding time zone, a time zone leading up to the current time. The key idea of the perfect, therefore, is 'beforeness'. Contrast, for example:

She *works* in a hospital.       (at the present time)
She *has worked* in a hospital.   (at some time in the past)

The perfect combines with **modal auxiliaries**, for example *may have arrived*, *could have disappeared*. With *will*, it typically refers to a time seen in the past from a point in the future ('past in the future'): *By tomorrow evening, the snow **will have disappeared***. The perfect can also combine with **progressive** (perfect progressive) and **passive** constructions, and occurs in **non-finite** verb phrases (perfect **infinitive** and *-ing* phrases). Table 3 illustrates the main types of verb phrase in which the perfect occurs. (See also **present perfect; past perfect**.)

*Table 3*  Main types of verb phrase in which the perfect occurs

| Finite | Present perfect | Past perfect |
|---|---|---|
| Perfect simple | has eaten<br>has mended | had eaten<br>had mended |
| Perfect progressive | has been eating<br>has been mending | had been eating<br>had been mending |
| Perfect passive | has been eaten<br>has been mended | had been eaten<br>had been mended |
| Non-finite | Perfect *to*-infinitive | Perfect *-ing* phrase |
| Perfect simple | to have eaten<br>to have mended | having eaten<br>having mended |
| Perfect progressive | to have been eating<br>to have been mending | having been eating<br>having been mending |
| Perfect passive | to have been eaten<br>to have been mended | having been eaten<br>having been mended |

**perfect infinitive, perfect progressive**    see **perfect**

**perfective and imperfective**    Two largely covert **aspects** of English grammar. 'Perfective' means that an event or action is perceived as a complete whole, whereas 'imperfective' means that it is perceived as something incomplete. The difference can be illustrated by this example:

| PERFECTIVE | IMPERFECTIVE |
|---|---|
| I *made* up my mind. | I *was making* up my mind. |

Here the difference is expressed by the choice between past simple and past progressive. However, in general, the non-progressive/progressive distinction only partially corresponds to the perfective/imperfective one. As aspectual terms, perfective and **perfect** are quite different categories, although (confusingly) 'perfective' is sometimes used as a synonym for 'perfect'.

**person**   A grammatical category which applies primarily to pronouns and secondarily to noun phrases and verbs. **Personal pronouns** and **reflexive pronouns** are classed as first person (*I, we, ours, ourselves, us*), second person (*you, yours, yourself*) or third person (*she, he, it, they, herself* and so on). First person pronouns refer to the speaker (or, in the plural, to the speaker and other people). Second person pronouns refer to the hearer, with or without other people, but excluding the speaker. The third person refers to people, things and so on, excluding both the speaker and the hearer. Apart from pronouns, person plays a role in the choice of the **finite verb**. The *-s* form of the verb (for example, *takes, likes*) follows a third-person singular subject (*he/she/it* **takes**), whereas the base form is used for first and second person singular, as well as all plural subjects (*I/you/they* **like**). Apart from personal pronouns, all other noun phrases are third person (*The cat* **likes** *fish. The cats* **like** *fish*). (See **personal pronouns; reflexive pronouns; number.**)

**personal pronouns**   The most important class of pronouns, referring to people, things, events and so on which are understood to be known in the context. Personal pronouns frequently have an **antecedent**, that is an expression to which they refer (or, strictly, corefer) in the preceding or following context. For example, in *Carol tells me she is changing her job*, *she* and *her* most likely (though not inevitably) refer to Carol, who has been mentioned in the subject of the sentence. Personal pronouns vary on four dimensions: **number, person, case** and **gender**, as shown in Table 4. (See **case; gender; number; person; reflexive pronouns.**)

**phrasal verb**   A verb idiom which consists of two words, (a) a main verb, such as *take, find*, and (b) a prepositional adverb (often called a particle), such as *off, out, away*. Thus **take** *off*, **carry** *on* and **find** *out* are examples of phrasal verbs. Particularly

*Table 4*

|  | Case → | subjective | objective | possessive | |
|---|---|---|---|---|---|
|  | Number ↓ |  |  | 1 | 2 |
| 1st | Singular | *I* | *me* | *my* | *mine* |
|  | Plural | *we* | *us* | *our* | *ours* |
| 2nd | Singular | *you* | *you* | *your* | *yours* |
|  | Plural | *you* | *you* | *your* | *yours* |
| 3rd | Singular | *he, she, it* | *him, her, it* | *his, her, its* | *his, hers, its* |
|  | Plural | *they* | *them* | *their* | *theirs* |
| ↑ | Gender → | m, f, n | m, f, n | m, f, n | m, f, n |
| Person |  |  |  |  |  |

Abbreviations: m = masculine, f = feminine, n = neuter (or non-personal)

in informal English, phrasal verbs are common and numerous. Their meaning is idiomatic: we cannot easily infer what the expression means from the meanings of its parts. Thus **take** *off* (in one of its senses) means 'imitate' and **find** *out* means 'discover'. Phrasal verbs can be (a) intransitive (that is, not taking an **object**) or (b) transitive (that is, taking an object):

(a) As one aircraft *took off*, the other one was *touching down*. (both verbs are intransitive)
(b) I asked them to *put off* the meeting, but they decided to *call it off* completely.
(both verbs are transitive, their objects being *the meeting* and *it*)

Notice that with transitive phrasal verbs, the position of the object varies. When the object is a **personal pronoun**, it comes before the particle (*call it off*). Otherwise, the object can occur either before or after the particle: *put the meeting off* or *put off the meeting*. (See **phrasal-prepositional verb; prepositional verb.**)

**phrasal-prepositional verb**    A verb idiom which consists of three words, namely main verb + particle + preposition, for example *put up with*, *look forward to*, *do away with*. (See **phrasal verb**; **prepositional verb**.)

**phrase**    A grammatical unit which may consist of one or more than one word and which is one of the classes of constituent into which simple sentences can be divided. The main types of phrase are **noun phrase, verb phrase, prepositional phrase, adjective phrase** and **adverb phrase**. Each is named after the word class (**noun, verb** and so on) which plays the most important part in its structure. (See **head; modifier**.)

**pied-piping**    Placing a **preposition** before a *wh*-**word** at the beginning of a clause or sentence:

> *From whom* did she inherit such qualities?
> The pub *in which the two men sat* had oak beams and brass horseshoes.

The origin of this curious term appears to be the story of the Pied Piper of Hamlin, who played his pipe and enchanted children to follow him, rather as the preposition may be imagined leading the *wh*-word as **prepositional complement** to the front of the clause from its normal position; compare: *She inherited such qualities from whom?*

**place adverbial, place adverb**    An **adverbial** (which may, for example, be an **adverb, prepositional phrase** or **clause**) which answers the question 'Where?', 'Where to?', 'Where from?' Examples include *here, to the meeting, wherever you want*. A place adverb is one of the adverbs which function as a place adverbial, for example *here, there, up, outside, forward*.

**pluperfect**    see **past perfect**

**plural**    The form of a noun, pronoun or determiner which indicates 'more than one', in contrast to the **singular**. For example:

|          | Noun     | Pronoun   | Determiner  | (Verb)   |
|----------|----------|-----------|-------------|----------|
| Singular | *student* | *he/she/it* | *this/that* | (*comes*) |
| Plural   | *students* | *they*   | *these/those* | (*come*) |

Verbs  are included in the table because they choose plural when their subject is plural. The regular plural of nouns is formed by adding -*s*, -*es* to the singular form. There are also irregular plurals: *man ~ men, wife ~ wives, mouse ~ mice, foot ~ feet, deer ~ deer, analysis ~ analyses.* Some irregular plurals coexist with alternative regular plurals: *people* or *persons, maxima* or *maximums, foci* or *focuses.*

**polarity**    The opposition between **positive** and **negative**.

**polysyndeton**    The use of a **coordinating conjunction** like *and* repeatedly to link **conjuncts**[2] in a coordinate construction, as in *all those duffel coats and jeans and badges and banners and open-toed sandals and push chairs and guitars and joints.* This classical Greek term, meaning 'many connectives', is the opposite of **asyndeton**.

**positive**    The opposite of negative; used, for example, of a clause or a sentence. (See **negation**.)

**possessive**    An alternative term for **genitive**, used especially for pronouns.

**possessive determiner**    The possessive forms *my, your, his, her, its, our, their* are sometimes called 'possessive determiners' because they occur in the determiner position, like *the*, in a noun phrase. Alternatively, they can be considered **possessive pronouns**.

**possessive pronouns**   A set of pronouns which correspond in meaning and position to **genitive** nouns or noun phrases. There are two series of possessive pronouns:

| (a) | *my* | *your* | *his* | *her* | *its* | *our* | *their* |
|-----|------|--------|-------|-------|-------|-------|---------|
| (b) | *mine* | *yours* | *his* | *hers* | *its* | *ours* | *theirs* |

Series (a) occurs in the position of a **determiner** in a noun phrase, like *the* (*My car's a Toyota*), while series (b) occupies the **head** position (*What's your car? Mine's a Renault*).

Their meaning can be one of 'possession' (for example, *my garden* = 'the garden which belongs to me'), but they can also have other meanings associated with the genitive, as in *their arrival, our hopes*. The first possessive form – (a) above – occurs in the determiner position, preceding the noun and any modifiers (for example, *their recent arrival at the hotel*). The second possessive form occurs in the position of a whole noun phrase, for example *My garden is tidier than yours* (= *your garden*). Like genitives, the second possessive pronoun can follow *of* in a 'double genitive' construction: *It had just been a romantic dream of hers*. **Personal pronouns** have possessive forms, as listed in (a) and (b) above, and in addition *who* has the possessive form *whose* and *one* the possessive form *one's*. The possessives contrast with **subjective** and **objective** pronouns like *I* and *me* in terms of **case**. (See **case**; **genitive**; **personal pronouns**.)

**postdeterminer**   A **determiner** which follows other determiners (especially **central determiners** like *the*, *this*, *my*) in the noun phrase. Examples of postdeterminers are *many* and *other* in *her many friends* and *the other day*.

**postmodifier, postmodification**   A **modifier**, for example in a noun phrase, which follows rather than precedes the **head** of the phrase. Thus in *the President of France*, *of France* is the **postmodifier** of *President*. The process of adding one or more postmodifiers is called postmodification. Compare **premodifier**.

**predeterminer**   A **determiner** which precedes other determiners in the noun phrase, including **central determiners** such as *the*, *this* and *my*. For example, *all*, *both* and *half* in *all/both/half the schools* are predeterminers.

**predicate**   The part of a **clause** or simple sentence which follows the **subject** and which consists of the **verb phrase**[1] together with elements relating to it. For instance, in *The boat arrived on time*, *The boat* is the subject and *arrived on time* is the predicate.

**predication**   The part of a **clause** or simple sentence which follows the **subject** and **operator** and which consists of the **non-finite** part of the **verb phrase** plus other elements relating to it. When its content is known from the context, a predication can be omitted by **ellipsis** or can be replaced by *do so*: *We have not yet sent you the order, but we will (do so) early next week.* (See **operator**; **predicate**.)

**predicative**   An alternative term for **complement**[1].

**predicative adjective**   An **adjective** which occurs in the position of **complement**[1], especially after the verb *be*, for example *tall* in *My sister is (very) tall*. Some adjectives (for example, *asleep*) are restricted to predicative use. Contrast **attributive adjective**.

**predicative complement**   An alternative term for **complement**[1], used by those who prefer **complement**[2] as the definition of 'complement'. For example, in *Commuting is a drag* and *Long hair is cool*, *a drag* and *cool* are predicative complements.

**premodifier, premodification**   A premodifier is a **modifier**, for example in a noun phrase, which precedes rather than follows the **head** of the phrase. For example, in *a Japanese custom*, *Japanese* is a premodifier of *custom*. The adding of one or more premodifiers to a head is called 'premodification'.

**prenucleus**   In an analysis where the **nucleus** of a clause is a **subject** + **predicate** structure, then a prenucleus is an element that precedes the subject, especially a fronted *wh*-**element**. In the following, *which* is in prenucleus position in the italicized relative clause:

It's really just a medieval romance, ***which I don't like anyway.***

**preposition**   A word which typically comes in front of a **noun phrase,** for example *of, in, with* in *of milk, in the building, with all the good intentions I had at the beginning of the year.* The noun phrase which follows the preposition can be called a **prepositional complement** and the preposition together with its complement is known as a **prepositional phrase.** The prepositional complement may also be a **nominal clause** (for example, *He was ashamed of **what he had done**).*

In some circumstances, prepositions do not have a following prepositional complement, and they are then referred to as **stranded prepositions,** for example at the end of many *wh*-questions and relative clauses where the 'fronted' *wh*-word or relative pronoun has the role of prepositional complement: *What is this machine for? I'll ask the man I was talking to.* Prepositions include some very common words, such as *at, on, by, over, through, to.* In addition, there are quite a few **complex prepositions** which are written as more than one word: *away from, instead of, in front of, by means of* and so on. The meanings of prepositions are very varied, but two important categories are those of place and time relations: *at the airport, in the summer* and so on.

**prepositional adverb**   An **adverb** which is identical (or similar) in form to a preposition to which it is also related in meaning, for example *on, by, off, over, about, past.* (Words like *out* and *away* can be considered prepositional adverbs because of their close relations to the complex prepositions *out of* and *away from.*) Prepositional adverbs, unlike their matching prepositions, do not have a prepositional complement. For example, in *He jumped over the fence*, *over* is a preposition, but in *He jumped over* it is a prepositional adverb. Similar examples are: *She fell down the stairs* and *She fell down*.

**prepositional complement**  The grammatical element which follows a **preposition** in a **prepositional phrase**. Most commonly the prepositional complement is a **noun phrase** (which may be just a pronoun): *of the world*, *in my best writing*, *for her*. It can also be various other constituents, such as a *wh*-clause, an *-ing* clause or an adjective: *for what we are about to receive*, *on reaching the airport*, *in brief*.

**prepositional object**    see **prepositional verb**

**prepositional phrase**   A **phrase** consisting of a **preposition** (for example, *to*) followed by a **noun phrase** (or a **nominal clause**), for example *to my best friend*. Prepositional phrases have two important functions in grammar: (a) they can act as **post-modifiers** in a noun phrase (for example, *the oldest member of my family*); (b) they can also act as **adverbials**, specifying, for example, the time or place of an action or situation described in the rest of the clause: *The train will start its journey at midnight. It will leave from platform four*. (See **preposition**.)

**prepositional verb**   A verb idiom consisting of a **main verb** followed by a **preposition**, for example *look after*, *look at*, *decide on*, *consist of*, *cope with*. The choice of preposition is determined by the verb rather than by the independent meaning of the preposition. Prepositional verbs can be confused with transitive **phrasal verbs**, but they are clearly distinct in that the particle (or second word) of a prepositional verb is a preposition, whereas that of a phrasal verb is a prepositional adverb. The confusion arises because of the similar appearance of examples like:

I *looked at* the picture. (*at* = preposition)
I *looked up* the word. (*up* = prepositional adverb)

But the difference is clear when we note that *the word* can be moved in front of its particle (*I looked the word up*), whereas *the picture* cannot be place in front of its preposition: *\*I looked the picture at* is ungrammatical.

The noun phrase following a prepositional verb is sometimes called a prepositional **object**. Its role in the sentence is semantically similar to that of the object of a transitive verb (compare, for example, *I **looked at** the picture* with *I **examined** the picture*). However, this idiomaticity of ***look** at* does not prevent us from regarding *at the picture* in this construction as a prepositional phrase.

**prescriptive grammar**   The kind of grammar-writing that determines the rules of the language by what is considered 'good' or 'correct' grammar, rather than by observing the actual use of the language. Prescriptive grammar contrasts with 'descriptive grammar'. Two well-known examples of prescriptive grammar are the rules against ending a sentence with a preposition (*It's a rule no one can agree **with***) and 'split infinitives', where a word or phrase is placed between *to* and a following infinitive verb (*It's **wrong** to **even** think of it*). In practice these rules are broken rather frequently.

**present continuous**   An alternative term for **present progressive**.

**present participle**   A traditional term for the *-ing* form of the verb, especially when used in a quasi-adjectival way, for example *standing* in *the men **standing** about outside*. (See **gerund**; **participle**. Compare **past participle**.)

**present perfect** (or **present perfective**)   A verb construction which combines the **present tense** with the **perfect aspect**, consisting of *has/have* + *-ed* form (for example, *has received*, *have gone*). The present perfect refers to something taking place in a period leading up to the present moment:

(a)   I *have lived* in this place for nearly twenty years.

The present perfect therefore competes with the **past tense** in referring to past time. But note that in (a), *have lived* indicates a past state of affairs continuing up to the present, while the **past simple** (for example, *was*, *lived*) indicates a state of affairs that existed at a definite time in the past and which no longer exists now. Thus the present perfect is distinguished from the past simple as referring to the 'past with relevance to the present'. This 'present relevance' may be either a matter of continuation up to the present, or alternatively an implication that the effects of an event in the past exist at the present time:

(b)   My brother *has won* £1,000. ('He has the money now')
(c)   Poor Mary *has injured* her arm. ('Her arm is still bad')

Compare (c) with the past simple *Mary injured her arm* (*last month*), *but it's better now*. In some contexts, however, the past tense and the present perfect are both acceptable, and the meaning difference between them is not always significant.

**present perfect progressive**   A verb construction which combines the **present tense** with the **perfect** and **progressive** constructions: *has/have been* + *-ing* form (for example, *have been waiting* in *We have been waiting for hours*). This combines the idea of 'past with present relevance' with the idea of 'going on over a (limited) period'. In *I'm tired – I've been working all day*, it is the present result of a past activity that is focused. In *We have been waiting around for hours*, it is the continuation of the activity up to the present time.

**present progressive** (also called **present continuous**)   A **verb** construction combining the **present tense** with the **progressive**, and consisting of *am/is/are* + **-ing** form (for example, *is reading*, *are playing*). The present progressive, rather than the present simple, is used to describe events, situations or activities going on at the present time: *It's raining heavily outside*; *The home team* *are running brilliantly this afternoon.* The present progressive can also be used to refer to planned future happenings: *I'm playing golf with Sandy tomorrow.* Note, however, that verbs referring to states (for example, *be, know, seem, resemble*) do not go easily with the progressive. We use these verbs with the present simple to describe an ongoing state: *Terry seems tired this evening* (not *\*is seeming*). (Contrast **present simple**; see **progressive (aspect)**.)

**present simple** (or simple present)    A form of the **verb phrase** in which there is just one **verb**: a **present tense** form of the main verb (for example, *looks* in *This house looks very old*, or *look* in *These houses look very old*). The present simple is the most widely used form of verb phrase in English. It has a range of meanings with reference to present time and is even used occasionally for past and future events. But note that the **present progressive** takes up some of the 'semantic space' which the present simple has in other languages, being used for temporary happenings in progress or in prospect at the present time. Contrast, for example:

We *give* him money every birthday.
   (a general statement, implying that this is an annual habit)
We *are giving* him money for his birthday.
   (a specific statement, about what is happening this year only)

The interrogative and negative equivalents of the present simple (except with the verb *be*) require the use of *does/do* as a **dummy operator**:

What *do* you *give* him for his birthdays?
I *don't give* him anything.

(See **operator; present tense**.)

**present tense**    A form of the (finite) **verb** which contrasts with the **past tense** and consists of either the **base form** (for example, *come*) or the *-s* **form** (for example, *comes*) of the verb. The *-s* form is used for the **third person singular**; in all other circumstances the base form is used. The present tense generally indicates that what the verb describes takes place in a span of time including the present – but there are exceptions to this, such as the **historic present** (referring to the past).

**preterite (tense)**    An alternative term for **past tense**.

**primary verbs**    The three verbs *be, have* and *do*, which are the three most common and important verbs in English. The primary verbs function both as auxiliary verbs and as main verbs.

**pro-form**    A substitute form, that is a word or expression which has no detailed meaning of its own but has the function of 'standing in the place' of another (often more complex) expression. Personal pronouns are the most familiar examples of pro-forms. Other examples are the pronoun *one* (for example in *this one, a new one*) and the verbal forms *do* and *do so* (substituting for a **predicate** or a **predication**).

**progressive** (aspect) (also called 'continuous')    A verb construction consisting of *be* + *-ing* form, for example *is watching, were smoking, (will) be walking, (has) been writing*, in contrast to non-progressive forms like *watches, smoked, (will) walk,* and *(has) written*. In meaning, the progressive indicates something happening or in progress over a limited period. It also has implications of incompleteness: *I have washed the car* definitely implies that the job is finished, while *I have been washing the car does not*. (See **aspect; past progressive; present progressive; verb phrase**.)

**pronominal**    The adjectival term that relates to **pronoun**.

**pronouns**    A class of words which fill the position of **nouns** or **noun phrases** and which substitute for, or cross-refer to, other expressions. The most important class of pronouns is that of personal pronouns, which vary for **person** (*I*, *you*, *she*), **case** (*I*, *me*, *my*), **number** (*I*, *we*) and **gender** (*he*, *she*). Other classes are **reflexive pronouns** (for example, *myself*), **interrogative** pronouns (for example, *what*), **relative pronouns** (for example, *which*), **demonstrative pronouns** (for example, *this*) and **indefinite pronouns** (for example, *someone*). Pronouns function as the **heads** of noun phrases, and in fact usually constitute the whole of a noun phrase, since **modifiers** occur with them rather rarely. (Examples of modified pronouns are *poor little me*, *you yourself*, *what on earth*, *those who live abroad*, *someone else*.)

**proper noun**    A noun which is spelt with an initial capital letter and which refers to an individual (usually an individual person or an individual place). Proper nouns contrast with **common nouns**, which refer to classes of entity (for example, *boy* refers to the class of non-adult male human beings). Proper nouns do not normally have **articles** or other **determiners** (for example, *Thomas* is normal, *\*the Thomas* is not). Further, they do not vary for **number**: most proper nouns (for example, *Eliza*, *Kennedy*, *Athens*, *Jupiter*) are **singular** and a few (for example, names of mountain ranges such as *the Rockies*) are plural. In exceptional cases, names like *Kennedy* change their number and occur with articles (for example, *the three Kennedys*), but in these cases the usual view is that the proper noun (*Kennedy*) has been converted into a common noun, referring to a set of people with the same name (*Kennedy*). (See **naming expression**.)

**pseudo-cleft construction** (also 'pseudo-cleft clause', 'pseudo-cleft sentence')    A clause or sentence that consists of two major segments:

FIRST SEGMENT: a *wh*-**clause** (actually a **nominal relative clause**). SECOND SEGMENT: a **predicate** consisting of the verb *be* followed by a **noun phase** or some other constituent semantically equated with the first segment.

For example:

| FIRST SEGMENT | SECOND SEGMENT |
|---|---|
| What sickened me | was the smell of putrefaction |
| What you really need | is another credit card |

The curious name 'pseudo-cleft construction' derives from the similarity of effect between this construction and the **cleft construction** illustrated by *It was the smell of putrefaction that sickened me* and *It's another credit card that you really need*. The content of the *wh*-clause is treated as something already known or presupposed, and the other segment expresses some piece of new information contrasting with what might be otherwise supposed. There is also another kind of pseudo-cleft construction (called 'reverse pseudo-cleft') in which the *wh*-clause is placed at the end and the order is reversed: *Another credit card is what you really need.*

**purpose adverb, purpose adverbial**   An **adverb** or **adverbial** which adds information about the purpose or aim of an action: *in order that*, *so that*, *in order to*, *so as to* and *to* (+ infinitive) are all ways of introducing an adverbial **clause** of purpose. Purpose adverbials answer the question 'Why?': *Why did the Johnsons leave early? (They left early)* **to catch the last bus**. Words like *intentionally* and *purposely* can be considered purpose **adverbs**.

### Q

**question**   A type of sentence or clause which has an 'information gap' (for example, in *When did you post the letters?* the information gap is the time at which the stated event occurred). Therefore a question is typically interpreted as requesting information from another person. (But there are also questions – for example, **rhetorical questions** – which do not have this function.) Direct questions (see **direct speech**) end with a question mark (?). The major types of question are *yes-no* **questions**, *wh***-questions** and **alternative questions**:

| | |
|---|---|
| Are you going out? | (*yes-no* question) |
| Where are you going? | (*wh*-question) |
| Are you going out or staying in? | (alternative question) |

(See also **echo question; rhetorical question; tag question**.)

**question words**    see **intensification; interrogative; *wh*-word**

---

**R**

**raised constituent**    A constituent that belongs semantically to a clause subordinate to the one that it belongs to syntactically. For example:

(a)   [The place seemed deserted].
(b)   [It seemed [the place was deserted]].

(a) is a single clause, but in meaning, *place* is not the subject of *seem*. Instead, the following sentence (b) shows the logical meaning of the sentence more clearly. Here *the place* is the subject of the subordinate clause and has *was deserted* as its predicate. Hence we can say that *the place* is a raised **subject**. A different kind of example is:

(c)   [Ma expects me [to help her]].
(d)   [Ma expects [I will help her]].

Here (c) shows *me* as the **object** in the main clause, as we can see if we turn the clause into the passive *I am expected to help her* – where the corresponding pronoun *I* becomes the subject. However, in (d), which represents something like the logical meaning of (c), the clause *I will help her* is a subordinate clause expressing an expectation that is assumed to be in Ma's mind. We can therefore say that the main clause object *me* is a raised constituent – in this case, a raised object – as in (c) it belongs syntactically to a main clause, instead of being the subject of the subordinate clause as it is in (d). Raised constituents are possible only with certain verbs: for example, *seem* and *expect* in these examples are among the verbs that allow subject raising and object raising respectively.

**raising**   The rule or process that allows a constituent to be raised from a subordinate clause into a main clause. (See **raised constituent**.)

**reciprocal pronouns**   The compound pronouns *each other* and *one another*, which express the idea of a reciprocal relationship. Thus *Judith and Frederick waved to each other* means the same as *Judith waved to Frederick and Frederick waved to Judith*.

**reflexive pronouns**   A class of pronouns beginning with the form of personal pronouns and ending with *-self/-selves*. They are: *myself, yourself, himself, herself, itself, ourselves, yourselves, themselves, oneself*. Reflexive pronouns typically occur later than the **subject** and **verb** in a clause or sentence and are identical in reference to the subject: *Jacob injured **himself** playing football. I am not feeling **myself** today. Many authors write novels about **themselves**.* In an **imperative** sentence, *yourself* (singular) or *yourselves* (plural) can be used, according to the number of the implied subject: *Please make yourself/yourselves comfortable.*

   A second use of reflexive pronouns is for emphasis: *She herself cooked the dinner* means 'She, and no one else, cooked the dinner'. The emphatic reflexive pronoun is placed in **apposition** to another noun phrase – in this case the subject *She* – but may be separated from it for **end focus**: *She cooked the dinner herself.*

**regular plurals**   see **plural** (contrast **irregular plurals**)

**regular verbs**   see **verb** (contrast **irregular verbs**)

**relative adverb**   *When* and *where* are relative adverbs when they occur at the beginning of a relative clause: *the moment **when** the bomb exploded; the place **where** I was born.*

**relative clause**    A relative clause normally acts as a **modifier** in a **noun phrase** and gives information about the **head** or preceding part of the noun phrase (the **antecedent**):

> I've talked to the people [*who* live there].
> The computer [*which* they bought] was very powerful.

In these examples, (*the*) *people* and (*the*) *computer* are antecedents; *who* and *which* are **relative pronouns,** that is the words which refer back to the antecedent, linking the relative clause to it. The relative pronouns in English are *who/whom/whose* and *which. That* and zero introducing a relative clause are also considered relative pronouns according to one analysis, but according to another analysis, *that* is a **complementizer.** A **zero** relative pronoun or 'zero relativizer' is the missing element (a 'gap' marked below by Ø) which occurs at the beginning of a relative clause where *that, which* or *whom* could occur:

(a)  I'll comment on some of the points [Ø you raised].
     (= *which* you raised)
(b)  The people [Ø she works with] are very friendly.
     (= *whom* she works with)

The relative pronoun has varied functions in the relative clause. For example, in *which you raised* (a), *which* is the **object**; in *whom she works with* (b), *whom* is a **prepositional complement.** The term relative clause is also applied to clauses introduced by a **relative adverb.** Also, by extension, it is applied to clauses which contain a relative pronoun, but which have a whole clause or sentence as their antecedent: so-called **sentence relative clauses.** For example:

> They're always fussing over their pets, *which really annoys me*.

(See also **restrictive and non-restrictive relative clauses.**)

**relative pronoun**    A pronoun which begins a **relative clause** and which links it to the **antecedent** or head or preceding part of the noun phrase of which it is a part. The English relative pronouns are *who/whom/whose* (normally referring to people) and *which* (referring to things). Also *that* (mainly referring to things) and zero are sometimes considered relative pronouns (see **relative clause**). *Who* is a **subjective** form, *whom* an **objective** form, and *whose* a **possessive** form. (The **zero** relative pronoun is like an objective form – it cannot be used as **subject**.) The use of **whom**, however, is not common, and in informal English, *that*, zero or *who* is used instead. Here is a set of options, all of which are possible, although the last is less usual:

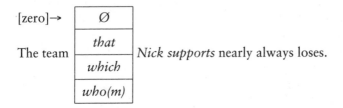

(The relative clause is in italics.) Compare also *the woman to whom we were talking* with the more informal *the woman we were talking to*. (See **pied-piping; relative clause; *wh*-clause**.)

**reported command**   see **reported speech**

**reported question**   see **reported speech**

**reported speech** (or **indirect speech**)   The language we use to report what someone else said, using our own words. Thus if Mary said 'I am sorry for John', someone could report this as: *Mary said **that she was sorry for John***. This is called a reported statement, because the original speech was in statement form. Reported speech is distinguished from **direct speech**, in which the original speech is repeated in the original words, normally enclosed in quotation marks. There are also reported questions. For example, if Mary said 'What did you say?', this could be reported by the hearer as *Mary asked him **what he had said***. And there are reported commands, requests or suggestions. Thus, if Mary said 'Please sit down' to Alan, this could be reported: *Mary* *told/asked Alan* **to sit down**. The following are useful 'ground rules' for reported speech:

(a)  It is normal to put reported speech in a subordinate clause:
   (i)   If the original speech was a statement, use a *that*-clause:
         . . . *that she was sorry for John.*
   (ii)  If the original speech was a question, use a **wh-interrogative clause**: . . . *how old he was.*
   (iii) If the original speech was a command/request/suggestion, use a **to-infinitive clause**: . . . *to sit down.*
(b)  If the original contained a **present tense**, change it to a **past tense**: . . . *was sorry for John.*
(c)  Where the original contained a **past tense**, use a **past perfect**: . . . *what I had said.*
(d)  Where the original contained a personal pronoun, change its person to the person appropriate to the situation in which it is being reported. Typically this will mean changing first- and second-person **pronouns** to the third person: *Mary said that she was sorry for John.*

Basically, these ground rules say: 'When you report speech, use the forms appropriate to your situation rather than the original speech situation.' They are not to be applied as mechanical rules because of detailed conditions that cannot be described here.

**reported statement**   see **reported speech**

**response form**   A word whose special function is in responding to the speech of another speaker. In English, *Yes* (or its informal variant *Yeah*) and *No* are the chief positive and negative response forms.

**restrictive and non-restrictive relative clauses**   A major classification of relative clauses (also called 'defining and non-defining relative clauses'). Restrictive relative clauses are so called because they restrict the reference of the noun phrase they belong to. For instance, in

> Summer holidays are a problem for most mothers *who have to work for a living.*

*who have to work for a living* is restrictive, specifying which or what kind of mothers. But if we insert a comma before the relative clause, it becomes non-restrictive:

> Summer holidays are a problem for most mothers, *who have to work for a living.*

This sentence now makes two separate statements: (a) that summer holidays are a problem for most mothers, and (b) that most mothers have to work for a living. Non-restrictive clauses do not restrict the reference of the noun phrase but add an independent piece of information about it. A non-restrictive clause has to have a *wh*-word (usually *who* or *which*) as its relative pronoun. It cannot have *that* or a zero relative pronoun. (See **relative clause; relative pronoun.**)

**result adverbial**    An adverbial specifying the result or outcome of the happening described in the rest of the clause. Result adverbials can be clauses introduced by *so that*, or *to*-infinitive clauses:

> Andy wrote very chatty letters, *so that she could almost imagine he was there talking to her.*
> I woke up *to find the house deserted.*

**rhetorical question**    A question which does not seek information, but rather implies that the answer is self-evident. *Who can say what will happen?* has the effect of a forceful statement: 'No one can say what will happen.'

---

S

**-s form**    The form of the verb which ends in *-s* or *-es*, for example *makes*, *wishes*, *adds*. The -s form is used when the **subject** of the verb is **third person singular** (see **person**): *She writes. He forgets.*

*Time passes*. The verbs *be* and *have* have the irregular *-s* forms *is* and *has*. (The *-s/-es* ending is also used for the regular **plural** of nouns.) (See **concord; number; plural**.)

**second conditional**    see **conditional clause**

**second person**    see **person; reported speech**

**second-person pronoun**    A **pronoun** which refers to the hearer/ reader (with or without other people, but excluding the speaker/ writer). The English second-person pronoun is *you, your, yours, yourself, yourselves*. As a personal pronoun, it has the same form (*you*) for **singular** and **plural**, **subjective** and **objective**.

**sentence**    The largest unit of language that it is the business of grammar to describe. In writing, sentences are marked by beginning with a capital letter and ending with a full stop (.), question mark (?) or exclamation mark (!). In spoken language, the definition of a sentence is problematic. There are no 'water-tight' definitions of the sentence, but it is useful to think of the **canonical** sentence as the largest unit of grammar, at the head of a hierarchy of grammatical units:

A sentence consists of one or more **clauses**.
A clause consists of one or more **phrases**.
A phrase consists of one or more **words**.
A word consists of one or more morphemes. (Morphemes are stems and affixes.)

Sentences may be divided into **simple sentences** – those with just one clause – and **complex** or **compound sentences** – those which contain more than one clause. If we restrict our attention to the simple sentence (for example, *The teacher corrected him amiably enough*), then we can talk about dividing the sentence into **subject** (*The teacher*) and **predicate** (*corrected him amiably enough*), or into elements such as **subject**, **verb phrase** (*corrected*), **object** (*him*) and **adverbial** (*amiably enough*). But strictly, these are components of the **clause** rather than of the sentence. The first stage of analysing a sentence, then, is to recognize whether it has a single clause, as above, or more than one clause, as in:

> [Today's weather will be fine], but [tomorrow will be cloudy and wet].
> [[Although today's weather will be fine], tomorrow will be cloudy and wet].

There are differences of opinion on how to deal with pieces of language that do not contain a complete clause and do not form part of a 'canonical' sentence, for example: *Good morning, Ben. Hi! From Dusk to Dawn. Oh my gosh. Sorry about that.* Such non-clausal units are not infrequent in writing and are extremely common in conversation. One solution is to call them **verbless** or minor **sentences**, recognizing by this terminology that sentences do not have to be defined in terms of clause structures. (See **complex sentence; compound sentence; sentence types.**)

**sentence adverb** or **sentence adverbial**   An **adverb** or **adverbial** which is peripheral to the clause or sentence it belongs to, and makes a point about the whole of the rest of the clause or sentence, for example: *As you know* in *As you know, I'm leaving my present job*; or *frankly* in *The play was disappointing, frankly.* Sentence adverbials can be divided into **conjuncts**[1] and **disjuncts. Conjuncts** are **linking** adverbials which have a clause-, sentence- or paragraph-connecting function, such as *moreover.* Disjuncts are adverbials which imply the attitude of the speaker to the form or content of the rest of the clause/sentence, such as *as you know* and *frankly* above.

**sentence** (or **sentential**) **relative clause**   A **relative clause** that refers back to the whole of the preceding clause or sentence. In *Elaine keeps mice in her bedroom, [which is eccentric, to say the least]*, the part in parentheses is a sentence relative clause.

**sentence types** Sentences can be classified into basic types according to their meaning and function in discourse. The four types that are traditionally recognized, in order of importance, are **statements, questions, commands** (or directive sentences) and **exclamations**). A single compound sentence can sometimes include more than one of these types. The following combines a command and a statement:

[Leave the building immediately,] or [I'll summon the police].

It is common to classify clauses into a similar set of types: **declarative, interrogative, imperative** and **exclamative**, so that, for example, a question and an interrogative clause mean more or less the same thing. There is a difference, however, in that terms for sentence types tend to be interpreted according to their meaning or function, while terms for clause types tend to be interpreted according to their grammatical form. There are quite a few mismatches. For instance,

| | |
|---|---|
| *Will you shut the door* | is interrogative in form, but a command in function |
| *You're not leaving?* | is declarative in form, but a question in function |
| *Officers will report to me* | is declarative in form, but a command in function |

(See **rhetorical question**.)

**sentential relative clause**    see **sentence relative clause**

**sequence of tenses** A kind of **concord** between the **tense** of the **verb phrase** in the main clause and the corresponding tense of a following verb phrase in a subordinate clause. Most commonly it is a case of a past tense in a main clause being followed by a past tense in a subordinate clause. Compare:

(a) *I assume* [*you are going to be late*].
(present followed by present)

(b)  *I **assumed*** [*you **were** going to be late*].
  (past followed by past).

The interesting thing is that the past tense of the subordinate clause can easily refer to the present time, as in *Hello! I didn't know you **were** here*. In such cases, sequence of tenses overrules the normal meanings of past and present tenses.

**simple past**    see **past simple**

**simple present**    see **present simple**

**simple sentence**    see **predicate; sentence; subject**

**singular**    The form of a **noun** or **pronoun** used to refer to one entity or to something which is not countable, for example *tree, time, service, Louise*. See **number; plural**.

**specific definite and indefinite articles**    see **generic**

**statement**    The proposition expressed by a **simple sentence** in the **declarative** form (that is, where the subject is followed by predicate), for example: *Her secretary works upstairs*. Here *Her secretary* is the **subject** and *works upstairs* is the **predicate**. A statement can be negated (*Her secretary doesn't work upstairs*). Also, a statement can be either true or false, and is typically used to convey information. In these respects it contrasts with **questions, commands** and **exclamations**. It can be argued, however, that statements do not have to be expressed in a declarative form: for example, a rhetorical question, such as *Am I my brother's keeper?* has the force of a statement in **interrogative** form. (See **reported speech; sentence types**.)

**stranded preposition**    see **preposition;** *wh*-**clause**

**subcategorization**    This term generally refers to the way word classes like nouns, verbs and adjectives can be assigned to various subclasses or subcategories. Nouns, for example, can be classified as **count** and **non-count** or **common** and **proper**, adjectives as **attributive** and **predicative**, and so on. However, usually subcategorization applies to verbs, and the way in which verbs are subcategorized according to the type of **verb patterns** or **complements**[2] they take. For example, verbs are classified as **intransitive, transitive, ditransitive, copular** and so forth, according to whether they take (a) no complement[2], an object, two objects or a predicative complement. Other verbs are subcategorized according to the kinds of finite or non-finite **complement clauses** they take.

**subclause**    see **subordinate clause**

**subject**    The element of a **clause** or simple sentence which normally comes before the **verb phrase** and consists of a **noun phrase**. Thus, in *The play ends happily* and *Suddenly they could hear footsteps*, *the play* and *they* are the subjects, preceding the verb phrases *ends* and *could hear*. The subject of a clause can also be a subordinate clause: *[That he confessed to the crime] proves nothing*. Subjects can be recognized by a number of additional factors: (a) they have **concord** with the **finite** verb; (b) they are placed after the **operator** in questions: *Does the play end happily? Are these cars expensive?*; (c) they typically refer to the 'doer' of an action. This last factor, however, is unreliable: for example, in **passive** clauses, the subject does not refer to the 'doer', a role usually taken by the **agent** (if present) instead: *The show was praised by the critics*.

**subject complement**    see **complement**

**subject-verb concord**    see **concord**

**subjective (case)** (also called 'nominative')    The form taken by a personal pronoun when it acts as subject of a **clause** or sentence. The subjective **personal pronouns** are *I, he, she, we, they*. The pronouns *you* and *it* can be either subjective or objective. The pronoun *who* is a subjective *wh*-**word**, but it is also widely used in non-subject functions. (See **case**; **objective (case)**.)

**subjunctive** (**mood**)   A form of a finite **verb** sometimes used to express non-factual or hypothetical meaning. The subjunctive was formerly much more common than it is today. It survives only in three rather formal contexts: (a) the mandative subjunctive, in *that*-clauses such as *This committee will urge that the president resign his office*, expressing some kind of wish or plan for the future; (b) the formulaic subjunctive, as in *God bless you! Good fortune be yours!;* (c) the *were*-subjunctive, as in *If I were you, I would accept the offer*. In (a) and (b), the subjunctive is the **base form** of the verb, and contrasts with the *-s* **form** which is normal after a **singular subject**. In (c), *were* is used instead of the expected form *was* after a singular subject, to express unreal or hypothetical meaning.

**subordinate clause** (also called 'subclause')   A **clause** which is part of another clause, termed the main clause. Subordinate clauses are often classified according to their position or function in the main clause.

(a) **Nominal clauses** take on functions associated with noun phrases, for example subject or object in the main clause.
(b) **Adverbial clauses** take the function of adverbials.
(c) **Relative clauses** take an 'adjectival' function as modifiers in a noun phrase.
(d) **Comparative clauses** take a modifying function in an adjective phrase, an adverb phrase, or a noun phrase, following a comparative word or construction.

**subordinating conjunction, subordinator**   see **conjunction**

**subordination**   A method of linking or relating two clauses by making one clause subordinate to another. Contrast **coordination**. (See **subordinate clause**.)

**substitute form, substitution**     see **pro-form**

**superlative**     The form of a **gradable** word which ends in *-est* (or
*-st*), for example *oldest, longest, most, least*. The superlative
refers to the highest or lowest position on some scale of quality
or quantity, for example: *Mount Everest is the **highest** mountain
in the world. His mother's one of the **kindest** women I know.*
One-syllable gradable adjectives and adverbs form their superlative by adding *-est*, but for most adjectives and adverbs of more
than one syllable it is necessary to add the preceding adverb *most*
(or *least* for the opposite end of the scale), for example: *most
useful, most quickly, least important*. There are a few irregular
superlative forms, such as the adjectives/adverbs *best, worst* and
the pronouns/determiners/adverbs *most, least*. (See **comparative;
gradable words**.)

**supplementary relative clause**     Another term for a non-restrictive
relative clause. (See **restrictive and non-restrictive relative
clauses**.)

**syntax**     The part of grammar which concerns the way words
are combined into sentences. It contrasts with **morphology** (the
grammar of word structure). In English, most of grammar is
concerned with syntax because morphology is relatively simple.
For this reason, 'English grammar' and 'English syntax' are often
treated as more or less equivalent terms.

---

| T |

**tag question**     A short question which is added after a statement,
to elicit a confirming response from the hearer, for example . . .
*aren't you?, . . . isn't she?, . . . were they?* English has a broad
range of tag questions, whose choice depends on the grammatical form of the statement. The rules for forming the most
common type of tag questions are:

(a)  Copy the operator of the statement (using the non-con-tracted form), and change it to negative if positive or to positive if negative:

> She's pretty straightforward, *isn't* she?
> You haven't gained that much weight, *have* you?

(b)  If there is no operator, use the positive or negative form of the 'dummy auxiliary' do:

> She likes sugar in her coffee, *doesn't* she?
> The photos came out well, *didn't* they?

(c)  If the subject of the statement is a personal pronoun, copy it and place it after the operator in the tag question:

> We've met before, haven't *we*?

(d)  If the subject of the statement is not a personal pronoun, replace it in the tag question by the personal pronoun which matches its referent (in number, person, case and gender):

> The journey won't take long, will *it*?

There are other forms of tag question in English, including such invariant forms as *right? huh?* and *eh?*

**temporal adverb/adverbial, temporal conjunction** see **time adverb/adverbial; time conjunction**

**tense**    (1) The grammatical contrast between present and past forms of the **finite verb**: *look/looks ~ looked, take/takes ~ took.* Thus in English there are just two tenses: **past tense** and **present tense.** Notice that the **future** is not generally considered a tense in English. (See also **sequence of tenses.**)

(2) In a different mode of thinking common in English language teaching, the word **tense** is applied to combinations of tense and **aspect.** For example, **present simple, present progressive** (gener-ally called 'continuous' in this tradition), **present perfect, past simple, past progressive** and **past perfect** are considered tenses.

**tensed, tenseless**    Alternative terms for **finite, non-finite**

*that*-**clause**    A subordinate clause which begins optionally with the conjunction or complementizer *that* and fills **nominal** positions such as (a) **object**, (b) **complement** or – less commonly – (c) **subject** in the main clause:

(a)   He told me [that his mother was ill].
(b)   The trouble is [that I sing out of tune].
(c)   [That opinions will differ] is inevitable.

Note that in the post-verbal positions (a) and (b) the *that* can be omitted: *He told me his mother was ill.* But this is not possible where the clause is **subject** as in (c) (except where the subject is **extraposed** – see below). *That*-clauses normally have the force of a statement, for example in representing **reported speech** or thought. They can occur (with or without *that*) in the function of a prepositional complement, but then the preposition preceding them is omitted: in *I'm afraid (that) you will miss the train*, the *of* that would follow *afraid* in other constructions is omitted before *that*. *That*-clauses often occur as postponed subjects after introductory *it*: instead of (c), it is more usual to say, *It is inevitable that opinions will differ.* (See **extraposition**.)

**third conditional**    see **conditional clause**

**third person**    A third-person **pronoun** (or other third-person expression) is one whose reference excludes both the speaker and the hearer. See **person; personal pronouns; present tense; reported speech**.

**time adverb/adverbial**    An **adverb** or **adverbial** that adds information about the time of the happening described by the rest of the clause, for example *now, recently, on Monday, since I saw you last.* The commonest type of time adverbial answers the question 'When?' Two other types of time adverbial are those of

**frequency** (answering the question 'How often?') and of **duration** (answering the question 'How long?'):

| | |
|---|---|
| *Last Friday* we went to the park. | (time-when) |
| The phone bill has to be paid *every month*. | (frequency) |
| Why don't you stay with us *for a week or two*? | (duration) |

**time conjunction**    see **adverbial clause**

*to*-**infinitive**    The form of the verb phrase which begins with *to* + the **infinitive** (**base form**) of a verb. As the following examples show, the *to*-infinitive can be combined with the **perfect, progressive** and **passive** constructions:

| | | |
|---|---|---|
| *to go* | *to have taken* | *to be dying* |
| *to be seen* | *to have been eating* | *to have been caught* |

*To*-infinitive verbs are used to introduce *to*-infinitive clauses, a common class of non-finite clauses. The *to*-infinitive clause usually has no **subject**, although its subject is implied by the context. It may, however, have **objects, complements** and/or **adverbials**. Some of the variety of structures of to-infinitive clauses is illustrated by:

(a) I wanted   *to resign* (verb phrase alone)
(b) I tried   *to start* | *the motor* (verb phrase + object)
(c) He is said   *to have been beaten* | by the champion (verb phrase + by + agent)
(d) She aims   *to become* | *a doctor* (verb phrase + complement)

*To*-infinitive clauses can have varied functions in the sentence. They can be:

(1) nominal clauses (for example, as subject – including postponed subject in extraposition – or object of the main clause):

   *To have been beaten by the champion* is no disgrace.

It is no disgrace *to have been beaten by the champion*.
I have been wanting *to resign* for years.

(2)   adverbial clauses (especially as adverbials of purpose):

*To become a doctor*, you need to pass a lot of exams.

(3)   adjectival clauses (that is, similar to relative clauses):

This is the way *to start the motor*.

The subject of a *to*-infinitive can be expressed, if necessary, by using *for* + noun phrase:

It is no disgrace *for a novice to be beaten by a champion*.
What would be the best way *for us to contact you*?

Compare **bare infinitive.**

*to*-infinitive clause    see **infinitive; non-finite clause; reported speech; result adverbial;** *to*-infinitive

**transferred negation**    The placement of the negative word *not/n't* in a **main clause,** whereas logically speaking it belongs to a **subordinate clause:** *I don't suppose that Jill remembered the tickets*. Here *not* appears to negate the supposing rather than the remembering. But in fact, we understand the sentence to express a supposition that Jill didn't remember the tickets. Another construction favouring transferred negation is *seem/appear* followed by a *to*-infinitive: *He didn't seem to notice* is equivalent to *He seemed not to notice* or *It seemed that he didn't notice*. See **negation.**

**transitive verb**    A **main verb** which requires an **object** to complete its meaning. For example, the verb *make* is transitive, since the object cannot be omitted in sentences such as: *The new bakery on 4th Street makes excellent bagels*. (*\*The new bakery on 4th Street makes* is not a complete or acceptable sentence.) If no object or complement follows, as in *The first attempt failed*, the verb is termed **intransitive**. A transitive verb can normally be used in the **passive**: *Excellent furniture is made by this factory.* However, many verbs are transitive in one context and intransitive in another. Examples are *open* and *finish*:

| TRANSITIVE USE | INTRANSITIVE USE |
|---|---|
| Someone opened the door. | The door opened. |
| They have finished the game. | The game has finished. |

(We can add **adverbials** optionally after these verbs: *Someone opened the door suddenly. The game has finished already.* But this does not affect their classification as transitive or intransitive.) The object that follows a transitive verb may be called its 'complement', using complement in the sense of **complement**[2]. See also **ditransitive verb**.

**tree diagram**    A diagram used to represent the structure of a sentence (or some grammatical constituent of a sentence), in the form of an inverted tree. The term 'node' indicates a position on the tree and represents a structural unit. The apex of the tree, called the 'root', is typically the **sentence** node, and each node has one or more branches, shown as lines, representing the subdivision of a higher node into constituents. At the bottom of the tree are its 'leaves' or ultimate constituents: words or morphemes. There are different opinions over the best way to represent grammatical structure in the form of a tree diagram. Figures 1 and 2 below show two contrasting ways of representing the structure of the same sentence.

The abbreviations for constituents in Figures 1 and 2 are as follows:

Adv = **adverb**;               NP = **noun phrase**;
AdvP = **adverb phrase**;       PP = **prepositional phrase**;
Aux = **auxiliary verb**;       Prep = **preposition**;
Det = **determiner**;           VP = **verb phrase**.

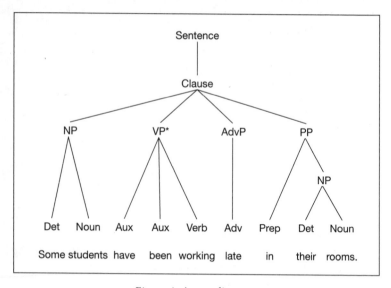

*Figure 1* A tree diagram.

\* The verb phrase in Figure 1 corresponds to **VP**[(1)] and the verb phrases in the second diagram correspond to **VP**[(2)] in the entry for verb phrases. The alternative labels for certain **VP**[(2)] nodes, **predicate** and **predication**, are added in parentheses.

## U

**unbounded dependency**    This is a rather difficult concept which is nevertheless important for explaining the power of grammar as an aspect of human language. A relation of dependency between two parts of a sentence exists when one part determines what can occur in the other part. This dependency is called 'unbounded' when there is no definite limit on the distance (in terms of grammatical structure) separating the two parts. As an instance, consider the ***wh*-question** in English. In a simple example, such as ***What did she drink__?***, the dependency is within a single clause. The *wh*-word *What* corresponds to a **gap** (signalled __)

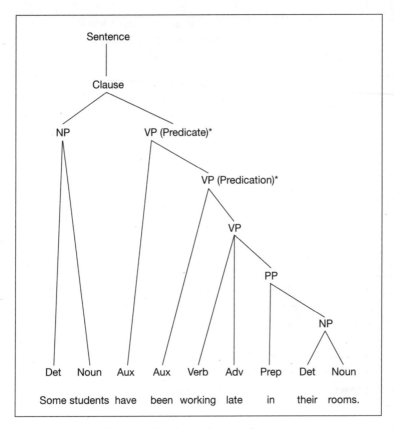

*Figure 2* An alternative tree diagram.

after the verb *drink*, where its object would normally occur. The dependency is evident when we notice that *drink* has to have an inanimate object. *Who*, for example, would not do as a *wh*-word instead of *What*: *Who did she drink?* In this case, the *wh*-word and the gap are in the same clause, but in other cases they can be separated from one or more clause boundaries (signalled by [ ]):

*What* did you say [she drank__?]
*What* did you say [they wanted her [to drink__?]]

*What* did you say [they wanted her [to start [drinking__?]]]
*What* did you say [they wanted her [to pretend [to start [drinking__?]]]]

Sentences could be made more and more complex by adding more subordinate clauses, but the complexity would never reach a stage at which the dependency between *What* and the gap ceased to exist. In this sense the dependency is unbounded. *Who* would still be unacceptable in the position of *What* in all the examples above. (See **catenative verb**.)

**uncountable noun**    see **non-count noun**

**universal conditional clause**    A clause which begins with a word like *whoever*, *whatever*, *whichever*, *whenever* or *however*, and which has an **adverbial**, **conditional** role in the sentence: *However old you are, you should take plenty of exercise.* The meaning is: 'It doesn't matter how old you are', or 'If you are *x* years old', where *x* can take any value. (See *wh-ever* word.)

**unmarked**    see **marked and unmarked**

**untensed**    Another term for **non-finite**

[V]

**valency**    A term with the same general meaning as **verb subcategorization**, **verb pattern**, **verb complementation**. However, **adjectives** and **nouns** can also have valencies. For example, one of the valency patterns for the adjective *tough* is that it can combine with *It* as subject and a *-ing* clause as complement[1]: *It's tough being a single parent.*

**verb**    A large class of words which indicate events and states of affairs, or which help qualify the reference of other verbs. Verbs are divided into two main classes: the class of **main verbs**, which has a very large membership (for example, *appear*, *drop*, *end*, *understand*, *revivify*) and the class of **auxiliary verbs**, which has a small membership of important verbs (*be*, *have*, *do*, *will*, *can*, *may*, *shall*, *would*, *could*, *might*, *should* and *must*). Of the auxiliary verbs, *be*, *have* and *do* are known as primary verbs – they can also act as main verbs. The remaining auxiliary verbs are known as **modal auxiliaries**. Except for cases of **ellipsis** (for example, *I can* said in answer to a question *Can you spare me a minute or two?*), almost every **clause** or **simple sentence** has a main verb. One or more auxiliary verbs can be added before the main verb, helping to specify its manner of reference, for example to specify **tense**, **aspect** or **modality**. With the arguable exception of modal auxiliaries, all verbs have a variety of forms. Most verbs are **regular verbs** and have four forms, for example *help*, *helps*, *helped*, *helping*. **Irregular verbs** (of which there are over 200) include many common verbs and all auxiliary verbs. The number of forms they have varies from one (the modal auxiliary *must*) to eight (the most common verb of all, *be*). The functions these forms perform in the verb phrase divide into those of finite and non-finite verbs, as Table 5 shows.

*Table 5* Functions of verb forms in the verb phrase

| Finite | | | | Non-finite | | |
|---|---|---|---|---|---|---|
| Present tense | | Past tense | Imperative/ subjunctive | Infinitive | *-ing* participle | Past participle |
| Base form | *-s* form | *-ed* form | Base form | Base form | *-ing* form | *-ed/-en* form |
| *look* *see* | *looks* *sees* | *looked* *saw* | *look* *see* | *look* *see* | *looking* *seeing* | *looked* *seen* |

Table 5 shows, first, the forms of a regular verb, *look*, and, second, the forms of an irregular verb, *see*. As a regular verb, *look* has the *-ed* form *looked* for both the past tense and the past (*-ed*) participle. But, like many irregular verbs, *see* has a distinct past participle form ending in *-(e)n*. (See **finite verb**; **irregular verbs**; **non-finite verb**; **verb phrase**.)

**verb complementation**    see **verb pattern; complement**[2]

**verb construction**    see **construction; modality; aspect; passive; verb phrase**

**verb pattern** (also called 'clause pattern')    A pattern which contains a main verb and whatever elements have to follow that verb to complete its meaning grammatically. For example, the commonest verb pattern in English is that of a transitive verb, which has to be followed by a direct object:

> **subject** (S) | **verb phrase** (V) | **object** (O)
> The council | has built | a new office block.

Note that *The council has built* is incomplete: something else is required, both grammatically and semantically, namely an object. The element(s) required after the verb is/are called the **complement**[2]/**complementation** of the verb. Using the symbols S (= subject), V (= verb phrase), O (= object), C (= complement[1]) and A (= adverbial) for the elements of clause structure, we can represent a number of verb patterns as follows:

| | | |
|---|---|---|
| SV | Jonathan's pet hamster \| has died | Intransitive verb |
| SVO | The chef \| is preparing \| something special | Transitive verb |
| SVC | Everybody \| is feeling \| hungry | Copular verb |
| SVA | Your travel agent \| is \| on the phone | Pattern with obligatory adverbial |
| SVOO | We \| should have wished \| them \| a happy New Year | Pattern with indirect object |
| SVOC | Meg's behaviour \| is driving \| her parents \| mad | Pattern with object complement |

Each pattern specifies what is required for completeness, but optional adverbials can always be added, for instance: *The chef is preparing something special **this evening***. There are many more patterns than these, some of them requiring subordinate clause structures as part of the complementation. They include:

| | |
|---|---|
| V + *that*-clause: | *I | imagined | Jane was lonely.* |
| V + O + *to*-infinitive clause: | *I | imagined | her | to be happy.* |
| V + *-ing* clause: | *I | imagined | meeting her in the street.* |

From these examples, it is also clear that the same verb (here *imagine*) can take a number of different verb patterns. (See also **phrasal verb; prepositional verb.**)

**verb phrase**  (1) A phrase consisting of one or more **verb** words. The verb phrase is the most essential and pivotal element of a **clause**. It consists of a **main verb** alone (a simple verb phrase) or a main verb preceded by one or more **auxiliary verbs**. (There can also be an elliptical verb phrase which consists of an auxiliary verb with **ellipsis** of the main verb.) The verb phrase involves five principal choices. The first choice, of tense, is between **present** and **past tense**, and involves choosing the appropriate form of the **finite verb**, for example *am/is/are ~ was/were; has/have ~ had; write(s) ~ wrote*. The remaining four choices are whether to use two-verb constructions and whether to use them alone or in combination. They are:

| | | |
|---|---|---|
| modal construction: | modal auxiliary + infinitive | *must eat* |
| perfect construction: | *have* + past participle | *has eaten* |
| progressive construction: | *be* + *-ing* participle | *is eating* |
| passive construction: | *be* + past participle | *is eaten* |

These constructions can be combined in the order stated:

| | | |
|---|---|---|
| modal + perfect: | modal auxiliary + *have* + past participle | *must have eaten* |
| modal + progressive: | modal auxiliary + *be* + *-ing* | *must be eating* |

| | | |
|---|---|---|
| modal + passive: | modal auxiliary + *be* + past participle | *must be eaten* |
| perfect + progressive: | *have* + *been* + past participle | *has been eating* |
| perfect + passive: | *have* + *been* + past participle | *has been eaten* |
| progressive + passive: | *be* + *-ing* + past participle | *is being eaten* |

And a further combination, namely of three constructions, is also possible though rare:

modal + perfect + progressive:
   modal auxiliary + *have* + *been* + *-ing*   *must have been eating*
modal + perfect + passive:
   modal auxiliary + *have* + *been* + past
   participle                                  *must have been eaten*
modal + progressive + passive:
   modal auxiliary + *be* + *being* + past
   participle                                  *must be being eaten*
perfect + progressive + passive:
   *have* + *been* + *being* + past participle   *has been being eaten*

Verb phrases can be either **finite** or **non-finite**. In finite verb phrases, the first or only verb is a **finite verb**, and following verbs, if any, are non-finite. In non-finite verb phrases (for example, *eaten, to eat, having been eaten*) all the verbs, both auxiliaries and main verb, are non-finite.

(2) In many models of grammar, the verb phrase is defined as a bigger unit, including not only the verb constructions above, but also the elements of a clause which follow the main verb such as its **object**. Verb phrase in this sense is equivalent to **predicate**. Another extension of the term is to apply also to **predication**. In fact, in such models, there can be series of verb phrases one embedded in another, so that all the bracketed [ ] elements in the following example are verb phrases:

The results [should [have [been [fed into Professor Lang's computer]]]].

(See also **passive; perfect; progressive; verb; verb pattern**.)

**verbal group**     Another term for **verb phrase**[1] – compare **nominal group**

**verbless clause/construction**     A grammatical unit which resembles a clause, except that it lacks a verb phrase. Verbless clauses are often clauses from which the verb *be* has been omitted by ellipsis: *A large crowd of refugees, **many of them women and children**, were imprisoned in the football stadium.*

**verbless sentence**     A unit of grammar that is independent, in the sense that it is not part of some other grammatical unit, and yet does not contain any verb. Although a verb is often considered essential to a **sentence**, verbless sentences are extremely common in spoken language and are far from rare in written texts. Examples are: *Happy birthday! The bloody key! How cool! No problem. Thirty pence please. Down! Yeah. More coffee? Entrance.* Other terms for verbless sentence are 'minor sentence (type)' and 'non-clausal unit'. It is also possible to argue that, if verbless clauses are accepted, an expression such as *Happy birthday* consists of a single verbless main clause.

**vocative**     A **noun phrase** (often a single **noun**) loosely adjoined to a sentence, identifying the person or people addressed: *Oh, **Thérèse**, I'd like to have a word with you. Well done, **you boys**.* Vocatives behave like sentence adverbials in that they can occur at the beginning or end of a sentence or even in the middle as in: *Come in, **Mr Wibley**, and make yourself at home.*

**voice**     The grammatical category which involves the choice between passive and active forms of the **verb phrase**. (See **passive (voice)**.)

### W

*were*-subjunctive    see **subjunctive**

*wh*-clause    A **dependent clause** which begins with a *wh*-word or *wh*-element. There are two major kinds of *wh*-clause: (a) **wh-interrogative** clauses, and (b) *wh*-relative clauses, including **nominal relative clauses**. A *wh*-clause beginning with the conjunction *whether* is a subordinate *yes-no* question, for example in reported speech:

> Europeans wonder [*whether the EU is ready for a common foreign policy*].

A *wh*-clause beginning with other *wh*-words/phrases can be a dependent *wh*-question:

> My mother never questioned [*what I was doing*].

An important aspect of *wh*-clauses is that they require the *wh*-element to be placed at the beginning of the clause, even if this means changing the normal order of subject, verb, object and so on. Thus it is common for a *wh*-clause to have the order **object, subject, verb phrase, . . .**, where the *wh*-element is the object: *I don't care **what you say***. In other cases the *wh*-element may be (a) a **prepositional complement**, (b) a **subject complement**, or (c) an **adverbial**:

(a)  It's a complex problem, [***which** we all have to live with*].
(b)  No one could guess [***how old** he was*].
(c)  It's a mystery [***where** those birds go in winter*].

When the *wh*-word is (the first word of) a prepositional complement as in (a), there is a choice between a formal and informal construction. The formal construction places the preposition at the beginning of the clause, whereas the informal construction leaves it 'stranded' at the end – compare (a) with the formal equivalent: *It is a problem [**with which** we all have to live*]. When the *wh*-element is subject of the clause, no change in the normal statement order is needed: *I can't remember [**who** lives there*].

*wh*-element   A phrase consisting of or containing a *wh*-word. *Wh*-elements normally begin with a *wh*-word. For example, typical *wh*-elements are *who*, *which chair*, *how often*, *whose car*. But one exception to this is the formal construction of a prepositional phrase in which the *wh*-word is preceded by a preposition: for example, *in which*, *for how long*. (See **wh-clause**.)

*wh*-*ever* word   A member of a class of words which resemble *wh*-words, from which they are derived by the addition of the suffix *-ever*: *whoever*, *whichever*, *whatever*, *wherever*, *whenever*, *however* and so on. *Wh*-*ever* words begin **nominal relative clauses** and **universal conditional clauses**: *Wherever you go, you'll have a ball*.

*wh*-interrogative clause   see **nominal clause; reported speech; wh-clause; wh-question**

*wh*-question   A question which begins with a *wh*-element: **Where** *are you?* **Who** *can we get to help us?* **How long** *have you been waiting here?* **Under what conditions** *have the prisoners been released?* Unlike **yes-no** questions, which strictly speaking invite only two possible answers – *yes* or *no* – *wh*-questions allow a large or open-ended number of answers. Compare, for example, *Is tomorrow your birthday?* (yes or no) with *What day is your birthday?* (1 January, 2 January, or . . .). As the examples above show, *wh*-questions typically require a change of the normal statement word order: (a) the *wh*-element is placed at the beginning, even if it is object, complement and so on, and (b) there is inversion of the **subject** and the **operator** (for example, *we can ~ can we*). There is no change of word order, however, when the subject itself is the *wh*-element: *Who said that?* (See **interrogative; question**.)

*wh*-word   A member of a small class of words which are **proforms**, filling a position at the front of a **question**, an **exclamation** or a dependent *wh*-clause, which can be, for example, an **inter-**

rogative or **relative clause**. Placing *wh*-words in initial position usually entails displacing them from their 'normal' position in the sentence. The *wh*-words are: *who, whom, whose* (pronouns); *which, what* (pronouns and determiners); *how, when, where, why* (adverbs). The **wh-ever words** *whatever, wherever* and so on behave in a similar way.

**word**    A basic grammatical unit which also largely corresponds to the main unit of the dictionary. In writing, words are marked as the smallest units to be separated by spaces. However, there is no 'watertight' definition of a word: many **compounds**, for example, are on the boundary of what makes a single word as opposed to a phrase. One useful criterion for words (as distinct from smaller units, such as roots and suffixes) is their relative independence in being inserted, omitted or moved around in the sentence. (See **morphology; syntax; word class**.)

**word class** (traditional term: 'part of speech')    A set of words which form a class in terms of their similarity of form, function and meaning. (That is, a word class is typically a meeting point of morphology, syntax and semantics.) The word classes which have a (very) large membership are **nouns**, lexical **verbs**, **adjectives**, **numerals** and **adverbs**. The word classes which have quite a small membership are **auxiliary verbs, determiners, pronouns, prepositions, conjunctions** and **interjections**. (See **open and closed word classes**.)

**word order**    This term is often used rather loosely to refer to the order in which elements occur in a clause or sentence. Within phrases, the ordering of words in English is relatively fixed: we have to say *a very old car*, rather than *\*an old very car*, *\*car old very a* and so on. Within clauses, however, the ordering of phrases as **subject, verb, object, adverbial** and so on is more flexible, particularly regarding the position of adverbials. Nevertheless, English is often termed a relatively 'fixed word-order language', because, compared with many other languages (and subject to some well-known exceptions such as the placing of *wh*-elements in initial position), the order of elements such as subject, verb and object is relatively inflexible. (See **end focus; end weight.**)

## Y

*yes-no* interrogative, *yes-no* question    A common type of **question** which invites the hearer to choose between two possible answers, *yes* or *no*. A *yes-no* question is closely related to a statement: in fact, it can be described as a question as to the truth or falsehood of a statement. It is usually distinguished from a statement (a) by word order and (b) by a rising intonation pattern in speech. To form a *yes-no* question from a corresponding statement, place the **operator** (that is, the first auxiliary or finite main verb *be*) in front of the **subject**:

| STATEMENT | YES-NO QUESTION |
|---|---|
| subject + operator . . . | operator + subject . . . |
| *You could wash the dishes.* | *Could you wash the dishes?* |
| *The clock has been mended.* | *Has the clock been mended?* |
| *The children are in bed.* | *Are the children in bed?* |

If the statement contains a simple verb phrase without an operator, the *yes-no* question must contain the appropriate form of the 'dummy auxiliary' *do* + the base form of the main verb:

*Sheila enjoyed the party.*      *Did Sheila enjoy the party?*

*Yes-no* questions can also be **negative**: *Couldn't you wash the dishes? Hasn't the clock been mended?* These are 'loaded questions', expressing surprise that the answer to the question is apparently negative. Another kind of loaded question is a *yes-no* question which keeps the statement order and relies on intonation to indicate its interrogative force: *So – you enjoyed the party?* This is a 'just checking' question and expects a positive answer. See also **tag questions.**

### Z

**zero**    In grammar, **zero** commonly signifies a word or suffix which is omitted and which leaves vacant a structural position in a phrase or clause. Examples of this omission are **zero articles**, zero relative pronouns and zero *that* (in ***that*-clauses** without an introductory *that*). (Compare **ellipsis**.)

**zero article**    This term is sometimes used for an **article** that is omitted before a common noun. The zero article is the normal way of expressing indefinite meaning before (a) a **non-count** noun, or (b) before a plural **count noun**, for example *water, trees*. The zero article contrasts with the definite article *the* (used for definite meaning in front of any common noun) and the indefinite article *a* or *an* (used for indefinite meaning in front of a singular count noun).

**zero plural**    An **irregular plural** of a **noun**, where the plural form is identical to the singular. English has a very few instances, including *sheep, deer, series, aircraft*.

**zero relative clause**    see **relative clause; cleft, cleft construction**

**zero relative pronoun**    see **relative clause; relative pronoun**

# Useful books relating to English grammar

This list of references gives a selection of books to be consulted and studied in following up the study of English grammar.

Under the topic of English grammar, there are many differences of terminology, theory and description. In the references below, I have used a * to identify publications with the kind of system of analysis central to this book, although there will be quite a few differences in detail.

Ballard, Kim (2001) *The Frameworks of English*. Basingstoke: Palgrave.

*Biber, Douglas, Susan Conrad and Geoffrey Leech (2002) *Longman Student Grammar of Spoken and Written English*. Harlow: Longman.

*Biber, Douglas, Stig Johansson, Geoffrey Leech, Susan Conrad and Edward Finegan (1999) *Longman Grammar of Spoken and Written English*. London: Longman.

Bloor, Thomas and Meriel Bloor (1995) *The Functional Analysis of English: A Hallidayan Approach*. London: Arnold.

Börjars, Kersti and Kate Burridge (2001) *Introducing English Grammar*. London: Arnold.

Burchfield, R. W. (ed.) (1996) *The New Fowler's Modern English Usage*, 3rd edn. Oxford: Clarendon Press.

Carey, G. V. (1976) *Mind the Stop: A Brief Guide to Punctuation*. Harmondsworth: Penguin.

Celce-Murcia, Marianne and Diane Larsen-Freeman (1999) *The Grammar Book: An ESL/EFL Teacher's Course*, 2nd edn. Boston, MA: Heinle & Heinle.

Chalker, Sylvia and Edmund Weiner (1994) *The Oxford Dictionary of English Grammar*. Oxford and New York: Clarendon Press.

*Conrad, Susan, Douglas Biber and Geoffrey Leech (2002) *Longman Student Grammar of Spoken and Written English: Workbook*. Harlow: Longman.

*Crystal, David (2004) *Making Sense of Grammar*. London: Longman.

*Crystal, David (1996) *Rediscover Grammar with David Crystal*, 2nd edn. London: Longman.

Downing, Angela and Philip Locke (2002) *A University Course in English Grammar*, 2nd edn. London: Routledge.

Givón, Talmy (1993) *English Grammar: A Function-based Introduction*. Amsterdam: John Benjamins.

Gramley, Stephan and Kurt-Michael Pätzold (2004) *A Survey of Modern English*, 2nd edn. London and New York: Routledge.

*Greenbaum, Sidney and Gerald Nelson (2002) *An Introduction to English Grammar*, 2nd edn. Harlow: Pearson Education.

*Greenbaum, Sidney and Randolph Quirk (1990) *A Student's Grammar of the English Language*. London: Longman.

Halliday, M. A. K. and Christian Matthiessen (2004) *An Introduction to Functional Grammar*, 3rd edn. London: Arnold.

Huddleston, Rodney and Geoffrey Pullum (2002) *Cambridge Grammar of the English Language*. Cambridge: Cambridge University Press.

Huddleston, Rodney and Geoffrey Pullum (2005) *A Student's Introduction to English Grammar*. Cambridge: Cambridge University Press.

Hudson, Richard (1990) *English Word Grammar*. Oxford: Blackwell.

Hurford, James R. (1994) *Grammar: A Student's Guide*. Cambridge and New York: Cambridge University Press.

Kennedy, Graeme (2003) *Structure and Meaning in English: A Guide for Teachers*. Harlow: Pearson Education.

Kirszner, Laurie G. and Stephen R. Mandell (1992) *The Holt Handbook*, 3rd edn. Fort Worth, TX: Harcourt Brace Jovanovich, especially chs 6 and 7.

*Leech, Geoffrey and Jan Svartvik (2002) *A Communicative Grammar of English*, 3rd edn. London and New York: Longman.

*Leech, Geoffrey, Benita Cruickshank and Roz Ivanič (2001) *An A–Z of English Grammar and Usage*, 2nd edn. Harlow: Longman.

*Leech, Geoffrey, Margaret Deuchar and Robert Hoogenraad (2005) *English Grammar for Today*, 2nd edn. Basingstoke: Palgrave.

McArthur, Tom (ed.) (1992) *The Oxford Companion to the English Language*. Oxford: Oxford University Press.

O'Grady, William, Michael Dobrovolsky and Francis Katamba (1998) *Contemporary Linguistics: An Introduction*. London and New York: Longman.

*Quirk, Randolph, Sidney Greenbaum, Geoffrey Leech and Jan Svartvik (1985) *A Comprehensive Grammar of the English Language*. London: Longman.

Radford, Andrew (1988) *Transformational Grammar: A First Course*. Cambridge: Cambridge University Press.

Radford, Andrew (1997) *Syntactic Theory and the Structure of English*. Cambridge and New York: Cambridge University Press.

Trask, R. L. (1992) *A Dictionary of Grammatical Terms in Linguistics*. London and New York: Routledge.

Trask, R. L. (1997) *The Penguin Guide to Punctuation*. London: Penguin.

Truss, Lynne (2003) *Eats, Shoots and Leaves: The Zero Tolerance Approach to Punctuation*. London: Profile Books.

# Suggestions for further reading

The number and range of books written in the last twenty years on English grammar is amazingly large and potentially baffling. Selection is difficult. However, all but three of the books in the preceding bibliographical list are intended for students or people without a specialist knowledge of or interest in grammar and I have classified them according to their particular focus or approach. The two main exceptions are the two comprehensive reference works mentioned in the introduction (Quirk et al., 1985 and Huddleston and Pullum, 2002), which are definitely not for the beginner. They are listed here not for their readability, but because of their influence on the teaching and study of English grammar throughout the world, which means that they are authoritative sources for terminology. As the present glossary locates itself mainly in the Quirk et al. tradition, this section begins with books which broadly follow the same tradition.

- Biber et al. (1999) is a detailed grammar based on a study of a large corpus of different kinds of spoken and written texts. This is a third important but not-for-the-beginner book.

- The following are student books using the Quirk et al. approach: Biber et al. (2002), Conrad et al. (2002), Greenbaum and Nelson (2002), Greenbaum and Quirk (1990), Leech et al. (2001), Leech and Svartvik (2002), Leech et al. (2005).

- Crystal (2004) and Crystal (1996) again follow the Quirk et al. approach, but are written more for the general reader and the teacher respectively. The latter book, in particular, is an entertaining read.

- As Huddleston and Pullum's comprehensive grammar is much more recent than that of Quirk et al., it has had little time to beget new offspring in the form of student books. But this situation has recently been remedied by a student textbook based on this model by Huddleston and Pullum (2005).

- Other good student books, not following Quirk et al. but taking a broad theoretically uncommitted line, are Börjars and Burridge (2001) and Hurford (1994).

- For those training to be teachers, Celce-Murcia and Larsen-Freeman (1999) – a 'bible' in the US – and Kennedy (2003) are important grammar books.

- The systemic functional approach of Halliday is well-represented for students in Bloor and Bloor (1995), Downing and Locke (2002) and Halliday and Matthiessen (2004).

- Other theoretical orientations are somewhat readably treated in Givón (1993), Hudson (1990), Radford (1988) and Radford (1997).

- For a more extensive coverage of grammatical terminology, enthusiasts can consult these dictionaries of grammar: Chalker and Weiner (1994) and Trask (1992).

- Other books worth consulting on English grammar, although they have a broader remit, are Burchfield (1996), Gramley and Pätzold (2004), Kirszner and Mandell (1992), McArthur (1992), O'Grady et al. (1998).

- Finally, I add three books on punctuation, which, although it is not covered in this glossary, is closely related to grammar: Carey (1976), Trask (1997) and Truss (2003). The last of these is added mainly – but not only – for its entertainment value.